"After Pat's Beatles' Show [...] him and his late partner to present the KQV Shower of Stars at Pittsburgh Civic Arena—so many great shows with the contemporary acts of the day! Over the years I was the MC and got to meet all of the luminaries of the music biz. One highlight was riding in a limo with Sonny & Cher to Greater Pitt after their concert. F-Bombs were flying in both of their tirades toward each other. Pat is a true show biz legend before my eyes and ears!"

—Charles Brinkman, Popular Top 40 DJ
and Music/Program Director

Pat DiCesare had a front row seat during the birth of the modern concert business. For decades there rarely was a show that passed near Pittsburgh that he didn't have a hand in. Concert promoters are often participants in amazing events with inside stories and tales of amazement that could never be told publicly if they want to stay in the business. Pat's now retired and lucky for all of us, he is now free to speak about his Hard Days in the industry.

—Gary Bongiovanni, Editor-In-Chief, *Pollstar*

"DiCesare's book has the stories you'd expect from a memoir about the legendary days of rock 'n' roll, from a madcap night with Sly Stallone to a rollicking, but tense, Janis Joplin performance in Pittsburgh. Along the way, DiCesare teaches the reader the intricacies of show business and about the complicated relationship promoters share with agents."

—Joe Reinartz, News Editor, *Pollstar*

"Pat worked with a great era of music, producing all the big shows. Reading his book brings back great memories of happy times from music all over the board."

—Chuck Blasko of the *Vogues* (original member)

"The first baseball stadium we ever played was a show promoted by Pat DiCesare. He was one of the only promoters we trusted to do big shows and we were right...through all the craziness...floods...insanity...he gave us and the fans a great night. Thanks, Pat!"

—Alice Cooper and Shep Gordon, talent manager

"Pat has 'seen it all'—I remember him so well from the beginning of my career to his amazing success as one of the 'legends of promotion' and, a great friend!"

—Tommy James, Tommy James and the Shondells

"Pat DiCesare was always there in the beginning. He had a creative force that helped so many artists. Thanks for the support and guidance. It was appreciated. Congratulations and best wishes for your continued success."

—Lou Christie, singer-songwriter, performer

Hard Days Hard Nights

From the Beatles to the Doors to the Stones...
Insider Stories from a Legendary Concert Promoter

Pat DiCesare

Headline Books, Inc.
Terra Alta, WV

Hard Days Hard Nights

by Patrick J. DiCesare

To order additional copies of this book or for book publishing information, or to contact the author:

Headline Books, Inc.
P.O. Box 52
Terra Alta, WV 26764
www.PublisherPage.com
800-570-5951

For more information visit www.ConcertPat.com

ISBN 13: 9781883568084

Library of Congress Control Number: 2014942910

PRINTED IN THE UNITED STATES OF AMERICA

*To my mother and father who gave me
the greatest gift of all—they believed in me.*

*To Tim Tormey, my mentor and partner,
who opened the door and showed me the
way through this crazy business.*

Foreword

This is the story of the birth of the rock 'n roll concert business, an industry that today runs into the billions of dollars run by large corporations.

When I started in the 50s and 60s I never would've envisioned the industry today. Back then, many of us early promoters never even knew there would be arena or stadium concerts, which of course became standard business.

Today it's hard to imagine that most people used to say, "rock 'n roll will never last." For the first time in the history of the world musicians with no formal training or education have, right or wrong, amassed greater fortunes than kings, more influence than presidents, and unfortunately, dare I say, more popularity than Jesus. The question "Is rock 'n roll here to stay?" doesn't even exist today, but back then entrepreneurs and businesses weren't willing to make the bet. Fortunately, I gambled and won.

I don't think anyone on earth would've bet on me to succeed in this business. I was the youngest boy of ten first generation Italian children who lived in a two-bedroom house in little Trafford, PA. Back then, everyone dreamed of getting a job in a steel mill or at Westinghouse Electric. I quit my job at Westinghouse to sweep floors and stock shelves at a record company, which is where my climb began.

When I started out promoters were splitting concert profits with four clean cut kids singing in tuxedos at a local dance hall for the weekend, and soon we found ourselves paying millions of dollars to demanding drug addicts in leather chaps and tattoo sleeves to play one stadium date to 60,000 screaming fans.

I must say that I've often longed for the days of paying the clean-cut kids as opposed to dealing with the likes of the unreasonable antics of some rock stars. Stories of demands of "no brown M&Ms" or 50 cases of booze amongst various other contract stipulations of eccentric rock stars have become legendary, and I lived them. They became a routine part of doing business. The trick back then was to please the rock band, their agent, and at the same time make the unholy seem normal to fans, parents, city officials, and arena/stadium officials. This was my life. This is the story of how we started the rock concert industry.

Chapter One
In the Beginning

We were poor but I never knew it—a big family struggling to survive the Great Depression.

My father emigrated from Italy in 1920. He and my mother had ten children, six boys and four girls. I was the youngest boy. They lost my oldest brother, Anthony, to crib death before I was born. We lived in a two-bedroom house. All of us boys slept in the attic, which had no heat. We froze during the winter, and sweated during the summer. My sisters all stayed in one bedroom on the same floor as my parents.

My maternal grandmother, the most lovable person I knew, lived next door with my aunt Angie and her brother, Uncle Joe. My grandfather died before I was born. We kids never wanted for much, but when we did need something (usually food), Grandma made it appear. She raised chickens, which were more like pets. When they were hungry, they would come up to her front porch and cluck until she came out with her apron full of scratch feed to scatter. Those chicks provided us with eggs and occasionally soup and a roast on holidays.

I was a lot younger than my brothers and I really admired their toughness and their ways with the ladies. Two of my brothers became Marines—to see them in uniform made me so proud. They were physically intimidating while I was thin and wiry. I was rather shy and I wished I could be confident and influential like them. I didn't think I ever would be.

My mother somehow fed all of us on my father's blue-collar salary from Westinghouse Electric. Our normal menu would have sounded weird to most American kids—rabbit, bacala, dandelions, zucchini, frittata, and pasta fagiole. Everything was homemade. Mum would buy twenty-five pounds of flour each week and make about twenty-five loaves of bread. We had pizza long before anyone knew what it was. We never had dessert except on special occasions, when Mum would save a little extra dough while making bread and fry it in oil. To make it really special she would sprinkle powdered sugar over it—if the budget allowed.

I hated lunchtime at school because the other kids brought perfect-looking sandwiches made with store-bought buns and Isley's chipped ham wrapped in perfect little packages of waxed paper while I brought peppers fried in olive oil and garlic sandwiched between two thick slices of Mum's homemade bread. The olive oil always managed to leak into the wrinkled brown bag and anything the bag rested on. Mum was a recycler long before it became fashionable, and we used those bags over and over.

We were different because we had less than the Americans (or the "Medigans," as my parents would say, referring to those who were born here). Dad came to America when he was 17 and learned to speak English here—he never allowed us to speak Italian. He would say, "You are Americans. You speak English." When Mum and Dad didn't want us to know what they were talking about, they spoke to each other in Italian. None of us kids had any desire to learn the language. We were Americans.

My Musical Career Begins

When I was in second grade, my father bought me a violin and insisted I take music lessons after school. Mum warned me to take good care of the instrument. "Your father paid a lot of money for that violin and we still owe Loreski's Music Store."

Almost every family had designated musicians to entertain at gatherings and to show off their brood's accomplishments.

After my very first music lesson, I was walking the three blocks to my home on Fourth Street. A group of older boys who were playing football began teasing me. After giving me a beating and breaking my glasses, they broke my violin. They called me a sissy for playing the violin when I should be playing football. That ended my career in music. For the time being ...

Six years later, my brother JuJu, who was a great performer and a heartthrob, quit school his senior year at Trafford High to join the Marines, leaving his accordion behind. My father thought it was time for me to resume music lessons.

Playing Bass for Uncle Joe

My Uncle Joe, who lived next door, had a band that played a mix of polkas, country, and old standards at clubs and taverns in surrounding towns. His three-piece group consisted of two guitars and a stand-up bass. He could play both guitar and bass, but he mostly played rhythm guitar and sang. One day when I was almost fourteen, he asked if I would be interested in buying his bass for $150. I had the money saved from delivering papers. I had no idea what I was going to do with such a big instrument, but since he offered to teach me how to play it and I was thrilled that he thought I could, I bought it. After I took the bass home, I realized there weren't too many songs that required only a stand-up bass.

After I took a few lessons, Uncle Joe informed me his bass player had quit and I would be replacing him. Sometimes I'd play accordion, too. We played every weekend at every fire hall, VFW, and wedding in our area. Uncle Joe paid me eight dollars a night—good money, when you compared it to the nickel a paper I made delivering newspapers. At fourteen I felt my musical career was starting to take off.

I never really knew if I was legal playing so young. Uncle Joe always told me to stay in the back of the band and stay in the kitchen during breaks. I played in his band for several years. I also started playing other jobs when Patsy Morocco, my schoolmate Bill's father, needed me in his band. I took lessons on any instrument I could get. I was fascinated by different instruments. I felt that I could talk to them and we'd become friends.

Eventually I quit playing in these bands to work at the most exciting thing ever—a job that was to lay the groundwork for my concert career.

The Holiday House

Near the beginning of my junior year in high school, in September 1954, I learned a new nightclub called the Holiday House would open soon in Monroeville, about ten miles from where I lived. When I heard they were hiring, I jumped at the chance to work there. After school, I drove three friends in my 1947 Chevy to Monroeville to put in applications.

We were told to go to the kitchen, which was filled with smoke and excitement. Men were working feverishly to add the finishing touches. It was the day before opening night, and the place was nowhere near ready. We walked past a worker yelling orders to another who was in a ditch connecting a sewer line. I asked him, "Where do we apply for a job here?"

"Go inside and ask for Edith."

After we filled out the application, Edith said, "Go over to that room and wait for Johnny Bertera, the owner."

A few minutes later, the guy who'd been working with the guys in the sewer ditch came over and said, "I'm Johnny Bertera." He instantly became my hero. He owned this organization, yet he would do whatever job it took to open in time. We all got jobs as busboys.

The next day we showed up for work in black pants, white shirt, and a black bow tie. The grill was producing a lot of smoke. All the doors had to be opened in the kitchen because the exhaust fans had not yet been connected. Everyone was stressed on opening day. It was an exciting type of stress that would last for all the days and nights I worked there.

I had never been to Vegas, but to me the Holiday House seemed the closest thing to that fabled spot. All the star recording and TV artists were scheduled to perform: Xavier Cugat with Abby Lane, Julius La Rosa, Buddy Hackett, Woody Herman, Tony Martin, Sophie Tucker, the Vagabonds, Phyllis Diller, Marty Allen, Eddie Fisher, and my all-time favorites, Johnny Puleo and the Harmonicats, "straight from The Ed Sullivan Show."

We worked two shows a night. Each show consisted of three acts—a dancer, a comedian, and a singer. Between the floor shows, the house band played music and the customers danced on the stage.

The minute I got out of school, I drove to the Holiday House. I usually worked until midnight weeknights and later on weekends. Each day after work I would go home, sleep, get up, go to school, and then head back to the Holiday House.

I soon learned the most important people at the Holiday House were the three Johnny's—Johnny Bertera, the owner; Johnny the head busboy; and Johnny the restroom attendant and spotlight operator.

Johnny the head busboy was in his thirties, which seemed too old even for 'head' busboy, but he took full advantage of his position. He was arrogant, egotistical, and just plain mean, but I had to be nice to him because he made the busboy work schedule and I was always afraid he wouldn't schedule me full-time.

Johnny the restroom attendant and spotlight operator was, I think, the only man of color who worked at the Holiday House. He worked in the men's room until show time, when he became the spotlight operator. He was helpful and always in a cheery mood that made you want to do anything you could for him. He was the calm amidst all the chaos.

As a child, I spent a lot of time next door with my beloved grandmother. She couldn't speak much English and I couldn't understand any Italian, but she taught me a lot, including how to work like "la machina."

I decided to become the best busboy at the Holiday House (and work like a machine). I was grateful to be getting 75 cents per hour plus tips, which I quickly learned how to attract. If customers wanted cigarettes, they'd usually give me a dollar. I'd get change at the bar and then run out to the cigarette machine in the lobby. I learned from the waitresses to put the pack of cigarettes on a plate with the change. The customer would usually pick up the cigarettes, which cost 25 cents a pack, and tell me to keep the change.

I learned to please the waitresses by constantly cleaning off tables, carrying trays of dirty plates from their stations to the dishwasher, and taking the trays, with covered dinners stacked high, from the kitchen line to the waitress stands faster than any other busboy. At the end of the night, they would tip the hard-working busboys in their sections.

The best customers—the best tippers—always got seats down front where they could "put their elbows on the stage." I knew I had to get into those sections, but Johnny the head busboy wouldn't put me there. He had his favorites and I wasn't one of them. My big break came when Irene, one of the oldest and best waitresses working down front, requested that Johnny place me in her station.

The most important person to the owner of the Holiday House was the chef, an older Greek gentleman named Jim. Johnny Bertera treated him royally. I quickly figured out that it would be a good idea to get close to Jim. I'd ask if I could do anything for him, and he'd tell me to scrub some greasy, grimy pots and pans. Nobody wanted that job, but I would do it, and the chef learned that he could depend on me.

Eventually it paid off. One day, Jim asked me to come behind the counter with him and do some short-order cooking. I grilled bacon and wrapped potatoes to bake in aluminum foil. Over time, he taught me how to grill steaks and to make my favorite, Turkey Devonshire. Even though I did all this work for him, he never spoke my name. In fact, he hardly spoke at all.

The chef didn't drive. This meant that one of the busboys had to pick him up at home and drive him to and from work. Johnny the head busboy usually got to drive the owner's new 1955 Ford Sunliner convertible (my dream car) to pick up and deliver the chef. Soon the chef asked the owner to have me drive him. That made me feel important, and I hoped it would give me a chance to learn about the business by talking to the chef. I got to drive Johnny's new convertible, too. The only problem was that the chef didn't like to talk.

The Eat 'n Park on Route 22 was on the way to the chef's home. It was a popular restaurant. Waitresses, usually high school cheerleaders, came out to your car to take your order and bring your food. The menu was mainly hamburgers, cheeseburgers, fries, milkshakes, and Cokes. As we drove past, Jim suddenly shouted at me, "I would rather own this Eat 'N Park than the Holiday House." I couldn't believe he was such a traitor. How could anyone not want to own the Holiday House? I was crushed. Jim was a great man, but I lost respect for him that night. How could he think any place was better than The Holiday House? I was crushed

The next day, I asked Johnny Bertera if he could find another busboy to drive the chef. I didn't want to hear the chef talk against the Holiday House again. So I lost two good friends that night—the chef and that Ford convertible.

The entertainers were booked by Georgie Claire, a licensed theatrical agent. He was a sharp dresser. He always exuded confidence and success. He had been a "hoofer," a professional dancer, who had an act with his wife. As he aged, he got tired of performing and became a theatrical agent. He liked to play poker at the prestigious Churchill Valley Country Club. At the time, I thought only the wealthy and snobby belonged to country clubs, so I thought Georgie was rich. I admired him, but he didn't even know my name. Nor did he know that his job booking the big-name entertainers was another occupation I desired.

Normally, an agent got paid 10 percent of an act's contracted price. This commission was added to the price of the contract. Johnny Bertera was too smart for that. He paid Georgie a flat salary of $200 per week. Back then, $200 a week was a lot of money. I was making only $30 a week, and my father was making only about $60 a week at Westinghouse. The agent had to be on call at all times. Georgie would play poker all day at the country club until Johnny called about problems or misunderstandings with an act.

I dreamed of having Georgie's job. What a life, to do such glamorous work and get paid so much. I wanted that job-- though deep down, what I wanted was to own the place.

We served no food during the show unless the kitchen was running behind. The headliners warned us not to clank any plates or glasses during their act (although we could get away with it during the opening act) so we didn't have a lot to do during the show. We could stand out of the way and actually watch the performance.

As the show was about to start, the band would quit playing. The customers would leave the dance floor. An employee would push the piano into place for the show and position the microphones for the upcoming entertainers. I loved being on the floor just before show time. I could feel the excitement build up as the house lights dimmed and the stage lights gradually brightened. The spotlight hit the emcee (the bandleader), who announced, "Ladies and gentlemen, Johnny Bertera and the Holiday House proudly presents..." The drum roll got louder and louder, ending with a flourish and a shotgun beat. The room grew dark as the spotlight focused on the opening act. Loud applause, band blaring. It gave me chills every time. I thought, "Someday I'll hear the emcee say, 'And now ladies and gentlemen, Pat DiCesare presents ...'"

Johnny the spotlight operator talked to the acts beforehand to learn their lighting cues. One day, he left a message asking for me to help him with the lights. I didn't know why. Usually Johnny, the head busboy, helped with this. But suddenly I was in the booth operating a spotlight and I was in heaven.

The next afternoon, I was told that Johnny the owner wanted to see me. I was nervous. What had I done? I'd never been in his office before. I knocked on his door. "Pat the busboy. You wanted to see me?"

"Oh. Yeah. You can come in, Pat." He looked up from his desk and said, "Pat, you've been doing a good job here. From now on, you're the head busboy. See Edie and she'll take care of everything. Okay?"

Did he say head busboy? I had to pinch myself. I had made it!

President for a Day

Even though my whole life now revolved around the Holiday House, I never thought of it as a permanent job. I was a conscientious student and got good grades, but I dreamed of more—much more.

I loved my hometown of Trafford, so-named by George Westinghouse, who built a large plant there in the early 1900s. After high school, I was expected to get a job at Westinghouse Electric, like everyone else in town. That was the ultimate security. You worked there until retirement. For most of us, college was not an option.

Miss Bierer, my homeroom teacher, was a highly-respected legend in Trafford who had been teaching there for ages. She was in charge of the English department and our National

Forensic League and she urged me to join the debate team. The debate team was a challenge I loved and at which I excelled.

At our first meeting of the school year, the team elected me president. I couldn't believe it. This was the validation I needed. It gave me the confidence I'd never had in school. My peers had voted me the president of the most prestigious club of all.

About the same time, I was visiting my classmate Bob Green, and his father said, "Pat, I think you should go to college to become an attorney." No one had ever told me that before. For the first time, I thought, *maybe I can go to college.*

I told my family about my new title. They didn't understand its importance, but they were happy for me. They could see how excited I was.

I was still beaming when I walked into my homeroom the next morning. Miss Bierer said to me, "Patrick, could I talk to you for a minute after school?" I was sure she wanted to discuss plans for the debating club. I couldn't wait! When school was finally over, I walked up to her desk and said, "Miss Bierer, you wanted to see me?"

"Yes, Patrick. In all fairness to the Debate team I think you should step down from the presidency and recommend that Gilbert Burkle take your place. He is more suitable. After all, Gilbert will be going to college and you won't. The presidency will look impressive on his admissions application." She said this so naturally, so matter-of-factly, apparently oblivious to my feelings.

I was crushed, but what could I say to a teacher who commanded so much respect? In that moment, my desire to accomplish something more in life than working at Westinghouse Electric died.

How would I explain this to my parents? My dad had only a fourth-grade education in Italy and spoke with an accent. My mother hadn't gone past the eighth grade. I certainly didn't expect her to fight my battle. Mum was an intelligent woman, but she was no match for Miss Bierer.

I decided not to tell them. I was used to solving my own problems. I never did tell my parents or, for that matter, Gilbert Burkle either. Gilbert did go on to college and medical school and he became a successful surgeon. Miss Bierer's confidence in him was not misplaced. But her lack of confidence in me was.

Chapter Two
Hard Days Hard Nights

"If you want the Beatles to play in Pittsburgh, take $5,000 in cash to the Club Elegant in Brooklyn and leave it with the bartender."

So now it was 1964 and here we were, Tim Tormey and me, with the opportunity of a lifetime in our hands—to promote the first Beatles concert in Pittsburgh. But we could see no way to make it happen. $5,000 cash was a fortune in 1964. It looked like the Pittsburgh Beatles concert was not to be ours. We had to have the money the next day. It was late in the afternoon and I was still at my distributorship. Wally, a small retailer from the South Side of Pittsburgh, came in and asked to see me in private. He looked nervous and he had two one-dollar bills in his hand. "This is for you. Take it." "What for?" I asked.

"Every time I order The Beatles records, your people tell me you're sold out. My customers are going to National Record Mart and Sam Goody's because I don't have any Beatles records. Sell me the copies you have hidden under the counter."

"Wally, I don't hold back records for special people. I don't care if they're for you or someone else. Take your two bucks back. When I get the next shipment in, I'll make sure you get some Beatles records. How many do you want?"

"Can you get me 25? I'll pay extra."

"I'll put you down for 25, and you don't have to pay me extra. It's still 60 cents for a 45 and $2.47 for an LP. Do you want any LPs if I can get them?"

"Can you get me ten?"

No wonder Wally was a small player. National Record Mart would have taken as many as they could get, into the thousands. It was a feeding frenzy—Beatlemania! Pressing plants were working overtime. Their latest record had sold 800,000 copies in ten days.

Retailers were offering to pay more money to beat their competition and get the records! But I never played favorites or charged extra. I did my best to distribute the records evenly whenever I got a shipment.

I said goodbye to Wally and drove home thinking "Where can I get five grand tonight?" Tim and I had done shows before, and I had promoted shows on my own. But this was The Beatles! And I was just a college kid!

I had taken a semester break to manage Regal Records for Tim, Nick Cenci, and Herbie Cohen. Even though Nick and Herbie were in business with Tim, they wouldn't advance the money. "Too risky," they said. It *was* risky, but $5,000 cash to get The Beatles was a reasonable gamble, I thought. I was willing to pay that.

I still lived in Trafford with my Mum and Dad. Dad usually got home at 5:00 p.m. from his job at Westinghouse in East Pittsburgh. By the time I got home, they would usually be finished eating. Mum would be doing dishes and Dad would be sitting in his favorite lounge chair watching the six o'clock news with his pipe, tobacco, and matches within reach. Both Mum and Dad would join me at the kitchen table. While I ate dinner, we would talk. That day, I told them about The Beatles and the $5,000.

My father, like most of his generation, didn't know whether The Beatles were a singing group, a car, or bugs on the back porch. I told him I needed $5,000. He didn't say a word. He just listened to my story. I don't think Dad had ever made more than

$100 a week working as a shipper at Westinghouse. In 1964, his paycheck was probably half that. He could never save money because he had nine kids to feed.

"Pat," Mum said, "why don't you quit that music business and go back to college and become a schoolteacher?"

Betting the House

The next day at supper, Dad slid an envelope across the tablecloth to me.

"What is this?" I asked.

"Go on, open it," he said. Inside was a cashier's check made out to me for $5,000.

"Dad, where did you get this?" I said. "You don't have that kind of money."

"I borrowed it from the credit union at work. They put a lien on the house."

I felt like crying. He'd worked hard all his life and still hadn't paid off the house and now he was offering me more money than he made in a year, all the money his home was worth. What if the bartender in Brooklyn just kept the money and we never booked The Beatles?

"Dad, I can't take this."

"Go do the show with your Beatles." He never brought up the money or The Beatles again.

I called Tim. "I got the money. Call Roz right now."

An hour later, Tim called back. "Roz said we can wire the money to an attorney if that will make us feel better. He'll take it to the bartender."

"Who do you trust more, an attorney or a bartender?"

Tim laughed. "It's a toss-up. But at least we won't have to drive to New York."

The next day, a depressing Pittsburgh snowstorm filled me with mixed emotions. I still had doubts about taking Dad's money for such a gamble, but I met Tim at the Western Union office on Smithfield Street and we wired the $5,000.

Walking out into the bitter cold afterward, Tim looked at me and said, "Well, partner, there goes your father's five grand. I hope we can trust that bartender."

The snow came down heavy and I had a sick feeling.

Tim and I were 50-50 partners. We had never had a contract, only a handshake. I never worried about him living up to his word. No banks or attorneys would endorse our way of doing business, but that was the way the concert business worked. And that was why no one else was willing to front the money.

The next week, The Beatles' agent, Norman Weiss of the GAC Agency, called and asked us to check out some open dates for September at the Civic Arena. Our gamble had paid off! The Beatles were playing Pittsburgh!

The date we were offered was September 14, 1964. We were carried away with excitement…until the agent informed us that the price would be a whopping $35,000. The most we had ever paid a headliner for a performance was only a tenth of that.

Tim negotiated the price down to $20,000 against 60 percent of the gross sales, whichever was higher. This was the first time I can remember an act receiving a percentage of the gate *and* a guarantee. The Beatles would make over $35,000 if the date sold out.

Meanwhile, the war in Vietnam was escalating and the draft was in full swing. While we were waiting for September 14, they drafted *me*. I got a notice to report to active duty at Fort Knox, Kentucky at the end of May. I would miss my own Beatles show!

Meanwhile, Tim and I agonized over the ticket price. Our prices at the Civic Arena had ranged from $1.50 to $3.50. The city imposed a 10 percent amusement tax, and there was another 10 percent federal tax on each ticket. So right off the top, 20 percent was gone. We were convinced people would pay more for this show, so we first agreed to a $6.60 ticket price. At that time $6.60 could buy you a gourmet dinner or a nice shirt. For the first time, doubt entered my mind; what if the Beatles couldn't sell out? What if we lost money? How would I pay back the $5,000? So we reconsidered and lowered the price to $5.90 to keep it from sounding astronomical.

It was the Public Safety Department that determined how many police officers should be on-site. The police chief insisted that we pay for 200 uniformed officers to secure the permit. For prior arena concerts we had needed no more than 20 officers. Tim negotiated the number down to 100 officers at $50 each. Tim insisted until the day he died that fewer than 100 cops showed, and some of them got paid only $20. Some of the cops working the show didn't really care about getting paid—they just wanted to be there.

Both the KDKA and KQV radio stations asked to be the show sponsor. KD was the big station in town, with 50,000 watts and several well-known jocks, including my friend Clark Race. They also had the biggest audience. When KD got behind an artist, they created hits. But they would never play our new artists' songs when we needed help to get a record started.

KQV had Chuck Brinkman, who hung out at Tim's office at the Carlton House every day and was begging for the show. When Tim met with Chuck's boss, John Rooke, Tim got everything he wanted. In exchange for the privilege of presenting The Beatles, KQV agreed to promote all of our future concerts on air at little or no cost to us. Every time we brought a concert to town, we would get the works. John agreed to play the artists' records and say things like "The Shower of Stars time is . . ." and "The Shower of Stars weather is . . . ." They would play our artists' records more frequently before a show. It was an amazing deal.

Normally, we sold tickets in advance at National Record Mart, but this show was different. Tim wanted to do mail-order only.

"How are you going to handle all the mail?" I asked.

"We'll have them send a self-addressed stamped envelope with their payment. I'll pay some nuns I know to mail out the tickets and deposit the money. Don't worry, we can trust the nuns. My sister is a nun in New York," he said proudly.

The Beatles concert sold out as fast as the nuns could handle the mail—all 12,600 tickets were sold in a day and a half, months before the concert. Now Tim had $75,000. He sent the Beatles their $10,000 deposit and sent me a check for $5,000, which I paid back to my dad.

One problem we could not solve was securing rooms at a hotel in town for the group. The hotels were afraid the fans would destroy the place. Secret arrangements were made for The Beatles to stay in Cleveland for three days and fly to the other cities where they performed.

On the day of the show, when The Beatles landed, about 4,000 fans were waiting at the airport. The police thought if The Beatles arrived early, they'd beat the crowd, but that was not the case. Their plan was to sneak the band in unnoticed, but with six police cars blaring their sirens the whole way from the airport, it was hard not to notice. Fans lined the streets to the Civic Arena as two limousines accompanied by six police cars delivered The Beatles.

The setup for The Beatles was amazingly simple. All their equipment arrived in a Ford Econoline van. Today it's not unusual to see acts touring with 30 semi-trucks and trailers and a dozen luxury tour buses. In 1964, we used the same sound system the arena used for sporting events for concerts. The hockey team's locker room served as a dressing room. To conceal the harshness of the cement floors and block walls and hide the lockers we had a reluctant Kaufmann's department store furnish and decorate the locker room. The store was afraid that its couches, tables, lamps, TVs, and carpeting would be trashed. But after the show, they sold their Beatles' dressing room furniture at a huge profit. The Beatles said it was the best dressing room on the tour!

Brian Epstein, their manager, thought The Beatles needed support acts. He certainly didn't need other names to sell tickets, but John, Paul, George, and Ringo wanted to save their throats to get through the 32-city tour.

The Fun Lovin' Five, which consisted of all the DJs from KQV, hit the stage first. They didn't expect to be paid. They just wanted to share the stage with The Beatles. But the audience didn't want to hear the DJs or the other opening acts-- Clarence "Frogman" Henry, Jackie DeShannon, the Exciters, and the Bill Black Combo.

They wanted the Beatles.

After the first act, a KQV jock came on the stage. "Let's hear it now for Clarence 'Frogman' Henry" he announced. The audience kept chanting, "We want The Beatles!" through all the other acts. When John, Paul, George, and Ringo finally took the stage, there was so much noise you couldn't hear them sing. In a half hour it was all over.

The Beatles' Share: $37,000

Usually, while a concert is in progress, the promoter is in the box office doing the accounting work with the arena, the city, the vendors, and the artists' representative. When the accounting was settled, The Beatles had earned $37,000 for their thirty-minute show, the most money we had ever paid an act. After all our expenses were paid, Tim and I split a profit of $8,800.

"What do you want me to do with your half?" he asked.

"Mail me $100 a month to Fort Sill. That will make me the richest soldier in the army."

My mother was still saying, "Pat, why don't you become a schoolteacher?" They were the only people who consistently worked during the Depression.

The year before, to satisfy her, I'd taught for a year at a Catholic school while I was in college. At Catholic schools you could work as a teacher before you graduated. After school and on weekends, I worked in the music business. As a teacher, I made $300 a month. In the concert business, I made $4,400 in one night.

A few years later, I was visiting Mom and Dad. I asked my mother, "What's the payoff on your house?"

She said, "I think it's around $3,500."

The next day I sent her a check for $3,500 with a note: "Thanks, Mum and Dad, for giving me the chance of a lifetime."

Oh, what a feeling!

A year after that, I was visiting them. We were sitting at the kitchen table, as we always did. Dad was quick to bring me something to eat. I slid an envelope over to my mother and said, "This is for you, Mum."

My mother was blind in one eye. She opened the envelope and saw a check made out to her and Dad. She said, "Oh, $50. Thank you, Pat. What's this for?" She brought the check closer to her eyes and said, "Oh, this is for $500. Pat, what is this?"

My dad looked closer at the check and said, "This is for $5,000."

My mother handed the check back to me and said, "Pat, you better not play around writing big checks. You could get yourself in trouble. Now take this back and stop this fooling."

"No, Mum, the check is good. Take it."

"What's this for, Pat?"

"Do you remember in 1964 when you got me the $5,000 for The Beatles?"

"Yes, Pat. You already gave us the $5,000 back. And you paid off this house."

"This is just a bonus, Mum. My way of saying thanks again for believing in me."

Oh, what a feeling!

I was now promoting every major act in the record business and making more money than I'd ever thought possible. But success took a long time and a great deal of work.

Chapter Three
The Civic Arena

In the summer of 1965 I was still riding the success of that first Beatles concert a year earlier. I'd been promoting concerts and getting to know the key players in town, including Charlie Strong, manager of the Civic Arena.

The Beach Boys

One day in July Tim called. He left Pittsburgh for New Rochelle, New York, at the beginning of that summer. "I want your opinion on an act I'm considering. Then I want you to check the availabilities for a concert at the arena for September 1."

"Who do you have?"

"I'll tell you, but don't tell Charlie Strong anything yet. Dick Clark wants me to put a national tour together with the Beach Boys as the headliner. How do you think they'll do?"

"They'll sell out everywhere. I like their music. They harmonize like the Four Freshmen but they rock. They write great music. I'll call Charlie now and see what's available. I really want the show, I'll call you right back."

I knew why he was asking. Anytime you put a show together you risk a lot of money--yours and everyone who becomes part of the show. I was happy to be one of Tim's confidants. People in the industry thought I had "good ears" and could tell if a new song was going to be a hit. I never thought that either Tim or Dick Clark could predict a hit, but I could, and calling me made

Tim feel a little more comfortable with his decision. This one was risk-free. I knew the Beach Boys would be huge.

"Hi, Elaine. This is Pat DiCesare. May I speak to Mr. Strong, please?"

"Certainly. He'll be right with you." Elaine Faith was Charlie's secretary and right-hand person. She was so efficient I always thought she could manage the Civic Arena herself. I liked her. She was excellent at her job and she respected me, despite my youth.

"Hello, Pat!" said Charlie Strong. "Now that you'll be taking over for Tim (who left Pittsburgh to work with Dick Clark in New York) I hope our relationship will be just as strong. He was a gentleman and I could trust his word. He tells me you're the same. What can I do for you?"

Charlie was aristocratic—he commanded respect. He always reminded me of Winston Churchill. "Well, sir, I need to set a date for a concert. Would you have September 1st available?"

"Is it for a musical?" he asked.

To me "a musical" meant a Broadway show with a musical score. Assuming he meant a music concert, I replied, "Yes, it's for music."

"What is the name of the show?"

"I'm sorry, but the producer didn't give me the name of the act yet. He just wants to know if the date is available."

"Well, I'd like you to stay away from any type that will cause trouble," he warned me. "But I will hold the date for you."

"Yes, sir, Mr. Strong. No trouble, just music." I felt like I was still in the service, saluting my commanding officer. I rushed to call Tim. "I'm holding the date. When will you know if we have a show?"

"Not so fast. Are you sure it will sell out?"

"I'm as sure as I was with The Beatles. It's that strong."

"Okay, I'll lock it in for you."

Tim and I had developed a way to roughly estimate our profit on a concert that sold well. If this show sold out, we could realize about a $16,000 profit.

I had to split with Dick Clark, since Tim was now working for him. I didn't mind that. I was happy to be Tim and Dick's partner. Dick never came to Pittsburgh when we had a concert, and Tim came only on occasion. But I had gone to New York a few times for meetings with Tim, Dick, and Jack Hook. Tim hired Jack because Jack knew just about every manager and agent in the business. We usually met at their office in Manhattan, but always ended up at Al and Dick's Steakhouse, where many of the record company executives, managers, and agents hung out.

On September 1, 1965, we played The Beach Boys at the Pittsburgh Civic Arena, where 12,392 people paid a total of $62,515 to see the show. The road manager was the son of movie star Dan Duryea, who played many B roles—but hey, he was a movie star. I was more impressed to meet his son than any of the Beach Boys.

The profit from the Beach Boys was even more than I'd made on The Beatles with Tim a year earlier. This was where I wanted to be! My agency business was doing great, as was a new chain of teen dances I had started called The Bug Out. For the first time in my life, I had a huge nest egg: almost $65,000 in the bank. I was on my way to making it big.

The Doors - After Miami

The Doors were not initially considered a controversial act, but Jim Morrison became notorious for performing "lewd acts," and indulging in drug-and alcohol-induced rants onstage. When I first booked the Doors back in 1968 for the spring of 1969, the worst thing he had done was sing, "Girl, we couldn't get much higher" on Ed Sullivan. Nobody really cared about that, except for the network. That changed in March 1969, when Jim was arrested in Miami for exposing himself onstage.

I'd first heard of the Doors in 1967 with their single "Light My Fire." I used to call Jimmy Grimes, the buyer at National Record Mart, to ask what the hottest-selling singles were, and

THE DOORS

Plus

The Blues Image

Saturday May 2,
Civic Arena 8:30 .

I often booked shows based on his sales reports. I didn't have to call Jimmy to know that "Light My Fire" was a big hit. It was still a hit two years later. The Doors probably could have sold out the Arena in 1969 even if their albums in-between had flopped.

The Doors had acquired a cult following on the West Coast. Thanks to the new phenomenon of FM stations such as WAMO and KQV in Pittsburgh that were playing album cuts along with singles, the Doors had a cult following in Pittsburgh, as well.

Usually, when booking a concert, I was contacted by an agent who ran through possible tour dates for several bands he or she represented. Bands like the Doors planned their tours around album recording sessions (unlike bands who had previously released only singles). I got a call one day from the Doors' manager, Bill Siddons, who was even younger than I was.

While he was attending college in Long Beach, California, Bill and two other students teamed up to promote a Doors concert at the school. It was 1967 and Bill was just a teenager. Jim Morrison liked the way Bill handled the show so much he asked Bill to manage the band. The last thing a manager wants is to see his act show up to an empty or half-sold venue in a strange city. In the fall of 1968 I had the Doors penciled in for the Civic Arena for Saturday, March 22, 1969. Bill made a friendly call one day. "Pat, I'm just checking in. How do you think we're going to do with our Pittsburgh date?"

"Bill, they're getting great airplay.'Light My Fire' is still very strong here. I checked with National Record Mart and I think we'll do very well."

"Do you think we'll sell out?"

"Yes. When can we go on sale?" I asked.

"Let's work out the numbers with the agency."

We put the tickets on sale in February.

A few months before the Pittsburgh date, an interactive theatrical show played in Los Angeles for a week. The actors ventured into the audience to taunt the patrons, the theater employees, and anyone else they could. It was part of the show. The more upset the audience became, the better the actors performed. Jim Morrison was in the audience on opening night and loved it so much that he went back every night for the entire week. He began to incorporate the casts' confrontational antics into his own show.

The Doors had accepted a date at the Dinner Key Auditorium in Miami, Florida, for March 1. When making the deal, Bill asked the new promoters for the capacity of the unknown venue, information he needed to structure the financial part of the deal. A fair deal at this time was a guaranteed amount to the artist and then a 60–40 split. The artist would get 60 percent of gross sales and the promoter would get 40 percent. Generally, the artist would allow the promoter to deduct certain expenses before the split, including any city amusement taxes.

In this case, The Doors would get a guarantee of $15,000 for the night and the promoter would get a profit of perhaps $5,000. Then, after deducting the other related expenses, the two would divide the remainder.

But in Miami, the venue had no permanent seating and there were no reserved seats. The Doors would have to depend on the word of the promoters, with whom they had never done business before, to determine how many seats were being offered for sale.

The promoters estimated the maximum capacity at 10,000 seats. On that basis, Bill Siddons accepted their $25,000 flat guarantee offer: So no matter how many seats were actually sold, the most the promoters would have to pay The Doors was $25,000.

On the day of the show, Jim Morrison traveled to Miami apart from the band. Bill and the other band members arrived at the Miami facility in plenty of time to have a sound check in the afternoon without Jim, who had not yet shown up. When Bill arrived and inspected the facility and saw that it could accommodate thousands more patrons than he had been told he confronted the promoters. They reminded him that they had a contract to pay a flat fee of $25,000. Bill realized that he should have specified in the contract that the $25,000 flat fee was based on only 10,000 seats. Bill told the promoters the fair thing was to pay the Doors based on the actual number of tickets sold. The promoters refused to comply and started making threats.

In the meantime, Jim had missed a connecting flight in North Carolina and was waiting at an airport bar. He didn't mind that too much and continued drinking until he managed to board another flight that would get him into Miami perilously close to show time. During the flight he continued drinking heavily. By the time he arrived in Miami he was in bad shape.

When Morrison finally arrived at the venue, Bill told him he believed the promoters were cheating them. The facility was not a regular concert venue. It had been oversold. The show was late getting started and the intense heat was annoying everyone. Bill was concerned for the safety of the people who were jammed into the overheated building way beyond the legal limit.

Normally, the promoter pays a 50 percent deposit upon signing the contract. The remaining half is due to the act on the night of the show before taking the stage. However, since Jim had earned a reputation for being undependable, these promoters didn't want to pay up until they saw him onstage and were sure that he was going to perform an entire show. Morrison was obviously intoxicated when he walked onstage.

When Bill went to the box office and demanded the balance of the money the promoters refused and warned him, "If you cause a problem, your equipment might get destroyed."

"Can you show me your ticket manifest?" Bill asked. That would prove how many tickets had been printed and offered for sale.

Again the promoters refused. "We agreed to pay you $25,000 flat! We don't have to show you anything."

This convinced Bill they were lying, but he felt there was nothing he could do. He sensed danger and thought the wisest move would be to get the show over with peacefully and get his artists out safely with their equipment, which they needed for the next show.

The crowd was restless, overheated, irritated, and tired of waiting. They expected a great show. But Jim was too tired and too drunk to deliver his usual great performance.

He began to mimic the Interactive Theater performances he had seen in Los Angeles, insulting the audience and the authorities. The audience booed. Jim retaliated by acting even more bizarre, taunting the police and everyone else in sight.

By now the police were congregating near the stage. The officer in charge walked onto the side of the stage with a few men. Jim taunted them even more. This was the worst thing he could have done because now the police felt threatened.

The danger escalated when Jim put his hands inside his jeans, shoved his finger through his open zipper, and simulated a sex act on guitarist Robbie Krieger. To the officers it appeared that Jim had exposed his penis, so they moved in on him and stopped the show.

Four days later, on March 5, 1969, the Dade County Sheriff arrested Jim for exposing his penis onstage, simulating a sex act, and inciting a riot. Jim and the band couldn't believe it. Nor could their manager, Bill Siddons, but Bill hadn't witnessed the performance because he was in the box office trying to get paid.

Guilty or not, Jim's reputation sank swiftly. Building managers and police departments in cities where The Doors were to perform became alarmed. Mayors were canceling permits for the shows. My own March 22 Doors show was turning into one of the most stressful dates of my career.

Finally, Pittsburgh mayor Joe Barr jumped on the bandwagon and forced me to cancel the sold-out show. I had to absorb the cost of advertising, promoting, and ticket printing costs and offer full refunds. Bill Siddons was kind enough to return my deposit. Charlie Strong at the Civic Arena understood my predicament and waived the cancellation penalty.

When the city finally let me present the Doors on September 20, 1969 I had to pay for almost as many police officers as we had for the Beatles Show. I was informed by the mayor's office, "If Morrison does anything immoral, we're arresting both of you."

For the September 20 date, I priced tickets at $4, $5, and $6--one of my higher-priced shows at the time--and we sold 12,234 tickets for a gross of $58,173.45. I made a promoter's profit of $14,000--not bad for the aggravation we all had to go through.

Fortunately, Jim behaved well enough to perform not only one but two Pittsburgh shows. The Doors liked the sound quality at the Civic Arena so much that they wanted to record a live album from a show on May 2, 1970, eight months later. I did so well with the first date that I agreed to bring them back for another concert.

After the Pittsburgh shows Jim moved to Paris. He was convicted in absentia on the Miami charges. He turned down an offer by a judge to perform a benefit concert in Miami in lieu of jail time.

Jim never served his sentence. Not long after the last Pittsburgh concert, he was found dead in his bathtub in the Paris apartment he shared with his girlfriend. He was 27 years old, the same age as Janis Joplin and Jimi Hendrix when they died. Two years later his girlfriend, Pamela Courson, committed suicide—also at age 27.

I've had the good fortune to meet many stars who appeared to have it all—looks, talent, fame, and fortune. After seeing what happened to many of them, if I had the choice of having fame or having nothing, I would prefer the latter.

Janis Joplin: Why the Fuzz, Man?

In the summer of 1969, I got a call from a New York agent who said, "Check on your availabilities at the Civic Arena for a Janis Joplin date."

I asked, "Is this Big Brother and the Holding Company?"

"Yeah, but Joplin is the star."

"I know they're big on the West Coast. But do you think she can sell out the arena?"

"Look, I need the date. It makes routing sense. Are you in or out? If you don't want it, I'll go somewhere else," the agent said. "Take the date. You'll make money."

In checking out an act before booking a date and negotiating the deal, the three biggest things I considered were my own ears, the reactions of trusted people, and the number of records sold locally. I could tell by peoples' enthusiasm when I named an act I was considering whether their show would be a sellout or not. If I told someone, "I have Janis Joplin coming to the arena," and they responded, "Oh, yeah?" I would be in trouble. But if I heard "That's great. When?" I knew the show would make money.

I was nearly $250,000 in debt from other losing ventures, so I took more of a gamble on Janice Joplin than I might have otherwise. Her song "Piece of My Heart" was not yet as big a hit in Pittsburgh as I would have normally wanted, but I felt certain by the concert date on November 1st, it would be.

I told the agent, "I'm in."

I figured if there were no unusual conditions, I could make $15,000 to $20,000. That would go a long way toward solving my financial problems.

KQV Presents
An Evening With . .
Janis Joplin
and Santana
PRODUCED BY
UNIVERSITY ATTRACTIONS
TONIGHT
CIVIC ARENA 8 P. M.
TICKETS $4-$5-$6
GOOD SEATS AVAILABLE AT ARENA BOX OFFICE

To diversify my business I had sunk about $90,000 into a Pittsburgh warehouse I converted into a concert venue called the Electric Theater where I could present psychedelic bands from San Francisco and other specialty acts. I'd invested another $100,000 in Rock Falls Park, a small amusement park in Slippery Rock, Pennsylvania. I was ahead of my time with the Electric Theater—a great facility that unfortunately never worked out—and I was bleeding green at Rock Falls Park.

The fallout got so bad I stopped answering the phone because it was always someone wanting their money—money I no longer had.

But I still had a great reputation with the agents. They rarely asked me for a deposit. Any new guy would have to put up 50 percent to get the act. The arena, the newspapers, and the radio stations would demand deposits, too. When you were doing as many shows as I was, this added up to a lot more money than I had. Tim Tormey taught me how to deal with all of these people successfully without spending my own money up front. The only deposit we'd ever needed was the five grand my dad put up for the Beatles.

To become solvent again, I needed the Joplin show to work.

Charlie Strong, the general manager of the Civic Arena, would come into his office early in the morning and stay for the show at night. I did the same, but I was forty years younger. Charlie was a great guy, but he could not accept the cultural change occurring in music. If performers deviated in style from the big bands of the 1940s, he considered them radical. During a concert, his assistants would run up to his office the moment anything he'd disapprove of happened, and he would get upset and come down to the stage. That served only to create confusion. He just didn't understand how to handle rock artists.

Rock stars *wanted* to whip the audiences into a frenzy. That was how they gauged their popularity. They wanted their fans out of their seats and in the aisles, dancing, clapping, and waving their lighters in the air. This drove the police and the firefighters crazy.

The afternoon of a show was usually hectic. The stress started with the roadies setting up. Roadies were always miserable, for various reasons. Often there were complicated riders on the artists' contracts. In the early days, we never provided the acts with food or drink. They were on their own—there were restaurants nearby where they could eat. But The Beatles changed everything. The acts started adding riders with all sorts of quirky demands.

At first the requests were simple, like bottled water. I first heard of Perrier in the 1970s when an agent said it was important for his artists not to drink the water in each city. He thought their stomachs couldn't handle the change in bacteria in the different water supplies and he feared they would get sick on the road. Not many stores stocked bottled water in those days. Most people didn't even know what Perrier was, and even fewer could pronounce it properly. But some acts demanded it.

Later, acts tried to outdo each other with their rider requirements. The best-known was Van Halens' "No brown M&M's" demand. Some wanted me to provide instruments, pianos of specific manufacturers and colors, sound systems, or dressing rooms painted a certain color. Guns N' Roses wanted a Roman orgy party. We had to find twenty good-looking girls to dress up in tunics and togas and stand backstage handing out bunches of grapes to anyone who walked by. The dressing room had to be decorated with concrete Roman gods and fountains. It cost me a fortune to comply with their demands, and I doubt they spent more than ten minutes in the room.

The Janis Joplin show was the first for which I had to provide a sound system. Her manager insisted that I use Clair Brothers from Lititz, Pennsylvania. Until then, every act used the Civic Arena's house sound system, which was designed for sporting events.

A few hours before Janis's show, Gene Clair, the eldest of the Clair Brothers, backed a 40-foot straight bed up to the stage door at Gate 5. I was standing outside the gate with his brother Roy and I asked, "What do you have in that big truck?"

"The sound system." The truck was completely filled with sound equipment!

In accordance with the stagehands' union contract only they could unload and assemble the equipment according to the artist's diagram. No one else was permitted to touch the equipment until the union workers were done setting it up for the sound check.

The stagehands unloaded the truck and I took Roy across the street for an authentic Italian lunch. At the end of the meal, Roy thanked me and said," Before we go to work, I want to give you a little after-lunch tip—get out of the concert business and get into the concert supply business. It's safer and there's no risk."

"What do you mean?" I was alarmed. Did he say to get out of the concert business? I couldn't do that.

"Look at us. You rent our sound system. Whether your show makes money or not, you have to pay us, right? Of course we want you to make money, but if you don't sell enough tickets, we still make our profit. You're taking all the risk."

"What concert supply business could I get into? You're already providing the sound. What else is there?" I asked.

"Stages," Roy said.

"Stages? Every arena and Theater has a stage. Who would rent a stage?"

"Stadiums. The future of this business is in ballpark shows. Attendance is going to explode. Arenas won't be able to handle the crowds. Go into the stage business now and you'll be the guy everyone has to deal with. You know all the agents. They'll all want you represent them. We're giving you great information here for the price of lunch.

"I don't know, Roy. Sitting in a ballpark for a concert doesn't seem right. No one would be able to see or hear. Who would want to go to a ballpark for a concert?" I asked.

"You'll see," Roy said.

Back at the arena the stagehands had diagrams showing where all the speakers were to go. I had never seen so many speakers for a concert—they were hanging from the roof, which was an amazing feat because the arena had a dome roof. The stacks were piled three wide and three high on each front corner on the stage. The mixing boards were bigger than anything I'd ever seen in a recording studio. We had to remove three rows of seats in the middle of the arena to accommodate them.

"Hey, Pat. I have to talk to you." The head usher, Whitey Riott, was turning red with anger. "What's all this fuss about the sound? They're blocking the view of people who bought seats. Where do I put those people? This is bullshit! Our house system was always good enough before. Why is Janis Joplin such a big deal?"

Roy Clair, who was by my side at the mixing board, said to Whitey, "Sir, you better get used to this bullshit. This is how it's going to be for all the bands from now on."

To produce a concert, you need a lot of personnel. The problem is you have to find good people willing to work part-time who you can trust. Most of these people were my friends, family, or people that already worked for me in other businesses.

At the time I had a theatrical agency, Pat DiCesare's University Attractions. Harry Popovich and Lee Smalley, my top agents, also worked as assistants at my concerts. I had many part-time workers, like my brothers Joe and Mike and friends Sonny and Chuncie Vaccaro. My brother-in-law, Joe Brown, was a great help, as were his brothers Timmy and Dennis, their friend J. R. McNeff, and my nieces Denise, Donna, and Karen. Charlie Robbins was my poster guy. I needed many runners who worked different shows, like Nicky Louvre and Steve Bogacki. I had different caterers for different acts, but my dad and brother Joe were the best.

We worked closely with the Shapiros, who owned National Record Mart. A part-time law school student—a friend of Bobby Shapiro's—handled all the rider requirements. Gerri Shapiro, the teenage daughter of Jason from National Record Mart, was a great assistant and secretary. Bob Miller, the business agent for the stagehands' union, was my contact between the artist's technical department and the Civic Arena. Bob was a capable person and since I rented additional lighting when needed, he worked cheap—only $25 per show plus his union wage as a stagehand.

Francis Dadowski and his brother, Bill, did all of my accounting, box office settlements, and payments to the artist management on the night of an event. This was the part of the business that I hated—and where I had to spend most of my time. I rarely saw my own concerts because I'd be in the box office working on the settlement with the artist's rep (who was generally a miserable person, probably due to stress put on him by the artist). It was my job to get the show on and over.

Before the Joplin show started, the backstage area was busier than usual. Janis was a sensation and everyone wanted to see her up close. Security was overloaded. There was more arena security than the excessive allotment of city cops I was required to pay, and I had my own T-shirt security, as well. There were stagehands, runners, teamster loaders, spotlight operators, sound crews, and clerks. Even the assistants had assistants!

They were all congregating backstage and I was constantly getting messages from friends, "Please, Pat, it's my cousin's daughter's friend. She came all the way from Buffalo to see the show. You have to let them backstage to meet Janis."

"Pat, here's a note from the mayor. His friends want to meet her. He says he'll never forget this favor."

"Chief of police's daughter,"

"Pat, it's me, Luigi. Tell her I'll do her hair—no charge."

"Pat, tell her to come over to my club after the show. I'll feed her some nice lasagna I made," Bridgette yelled. Everyone had an excuse to be backstage that night.

Chuncie, my assistant, came up to me at my usual spot in the main box office with John Woods, the box office manager. "Pat. Janice is complaining that she's gonna run out of Southern Comfort before the show even starts. What should I do?"

"For Christ's sake, Chuncie, did she drink the whole case?" I yelled.

"I don't know, but she said if you don't have more Southern Comfort, she's not going on. I gave her all we had."

"I thought you bought a case. Did you look in my car? Here's the key."

I had to get ready for Janis's road manager, who would do the accounting for her and would want to see the final settlement. I had to show the road manager the ticket manifest, which proved how many tickets had been printed. Then I had to produce the deadwood, the unsold tickets. The box office manager prepared an authorized box office statement that I had to countersign, which was used to verify the official number of tickets sold (and not sold). This statement was used as a basis to determine the Civic Arena's 10% cut for rent and the city's 10% cut for city amusement taxes. Using those figures, I had to produce another statement for the artist's manager, proving these and all the other variable expenses, so that everyone was satisfied with the final figures. Everyone was looking over my shoulder. Everyone wanted their piece of the pie. I couldn't cheat anyone even if I wanted.

There was a knock on the box office door. John Woods yelled, "Who is it?"

A voice through the door yelled, "Is Pat in there?"

"Yeah," John said, "Who wants him?"

"Harry."

John looked at me. "You want him in, Pat?"

"Okay." I could tell John was irritated because his work was interrupted and he would be pushed for time. We had to have all the accounting done for the act by intermission. Some managers or agents would refuse to let their acts go onstage if the accounting was not completed by the end of intermission.

John opened the door. "Dammit, Harry, this better be important," I said.

He was nearly out of breath. He must have run from backstage halfway around the arena. "Yes, Pat, it is."

"Well, out with it. Is she ready to go on? Do we have a show or are we in trouble?" You never knew with these acts, especially if the performers were drinking or on drugs. I never knew if I was going to have a show until I saw the act onstage— and even then things could still go wrong. The trick was to get the act on the stage and get the show over.

"She's fornicating with someone in her dressing room," he blurted out.

I looked up from the box office report that John had just handed me. "What did you say? And when did you start using the word fornicating?"

"You should come see."

"You ran all the way back here and interrupted us to tell me that? How do you even know?"

"Nicky heard them! The door was partly open and he looked in. Then he told Bob Miller. "Bob said she was fornicating," he said boastfully, as though he'd just solved a crime. He was beginning to catch his breath.

"What the hell is Nicky doing there anyway?" I asked.

"His job is watching the dressing rooms. If the act wants anything, he gets it. Everyone is looking," he said.

"I guess he'll want paid for doing that? He should be paying me. If I put an ad in the paper advertising that job, I could fill Three Rivers Stadium with the applicants. I don't care who she's screwing or where. All I want is for her to get up on that damn stage and get this night over. Now get the hell out of here. Tell Bob Miller and Bob Harper to get the show started. I'll be back there as soon as I can."

John Woods and I looked at each other. "Can you believe this?" I said.

I signed the box office statement and told John, "I'd better go back there and make sure this show gets started. If the road manager comes looking for me, tell him I'll be right back."

I was on my way to Janis's dressing room when I saw Chuncie Vaccaro. "Pat, I found the rest of the Southern Comfort in your trunk," he said. "She calmed down, but she's so drunk I don't know if she can stand up."

Oh, no. Why couldn't this night be over? Outside her dressing room, one of her guys said to me, "Are you ready?"

"Am I ready? I'm ready. Let's get it over with." I said.

"Yeah, man. Let's rock! This is going to be some show. I never felt the excitement that I feel tonight. Yeah, man, tonight is gonna be somethin' else." I wondered what that meant.

Janis literally wobbled out of her dressing room. I said hello, then followed her and the band up the stairs to the top of the stage. She was wearing fishnet see-through clothing with no underwear. Once she was actually onstage, I felt relieved. The profit from this night would pay down my debt. All I had to do was get the show over.

The crowd was seething with anticipation. When the spotlight hit Janis you could see *everything*; it was as though she wore no clothing. The crowd loved her as she started out with a monologue. She was the first female performer I ever heard use the F word onstage, and she wasn't bashful about it. The audience responded with enthusiasm for her unique vocabulary.

Once the show started, I went back to the box office to settle the show with the road manager. I would pay him the money due Janis from the percentage of tickets sold. In 45 minutes the concert would be over and I'd have my money.

We were about 25 minutes into her show when Charlie got the news from his stoolies that she was swearing onstage. He came down from his office. He wanted to turn the lights on in the auditorium and turn the sound off on Janis. When I got the call that he was backstage, I was still in the box office. I told Richard Irace with Civic Arena security to tell Charlie not to do anything until I got there. Running all the way, I arrived backstage to find Charlie telling police sergeant Jim Patterson, "Get that girl off stage and down here right now. I'm going to wash her mouth out with soap. We're going to stop this show until she learns to behave herself."

Jim snapped back, "Mr. Strong, you aren't going to do anything of the kind. You shouldn't even be here. Get with the times."

I pleaded, "Charlie, whatever you do, don't cut the sound or turn on the lights while she's performing."

Janis had the house rocking. Everyone was standing. The aisles were jammed and the fans were all pushing towards the stage. To Charlie, the situation was out of control.

"Charlie, in a half hour the show will be over. Everyone will go home. But if you stop the show now there could be a riot. They could tear the arena apart, throw chairs, rush the stage, and fight with your security. People will get hurt."

"I'm going to go up there and wash her mouth out with soap," he repeated.

"Mr. Strong, shut up and go back to your office, we'll take care of this." Jim Patterson demanded. "We'll take care of this." Then he said to me, "Can *you* go up onstage and talk to her?"

"Talk to her?" I shouted into his ear. "Jim, this is what she wants. I assure you, there won't be a problem if we just let her finish the show. So what if the audience is on their feet?"

"Let's go up on the stage," said Jim. "If there is a problem, we'll have a better chance to do something about it." The music was pulsating as Jim, Charlie, and I walked up the steps at the back of the arena stage.

Charlie yelled, "Why is she so loud? I've never heard a performer sing so loud. And that music! It's terrible."

I tried to explain to Charlie, this is not the 1940s anymore. In the fifties, when acts like the Coasters and the Drifters became popular, some people thought their music was too loud. Now, it was the late sixties and the, music *had* to be loud. Now audiences wanted to *feel* the sound as well as hear it.

Why the Fuzz, Man?

Once Jim, Charlie, and I were onstage, Janis couldn't see us. Neither could the audience. We stood behind the large amps in the back. A roadie ran over to me, grabbed my arm, and said "What the fuck are you doing here? And why the fuzz, man?"

"Be cool, nothing's happening. They're just checking things out," I said.

"What about the fuzz, man? What's happening? Don't go doing anything stupid."

Charlie came running from behind the amps onto the stage. Things were getting worse. Janis would swear and the crowd loved it. They'd swear back. Then she'd take a swig of Southern Comfort straight out of the bottle and say, "Fuckin' good shit." The more bizarre she acted, the wilder they became. I had to admit, it was getting out of hand. The crowd kept pushing toward the stage, and some kids were so crushed against the stage that they couldn't move. I was getting worried. But the show was almost over. If we could get her to sing her hit, we could end the show. She had to sing "Piece of My Heart."

The crowd was encouraging her to drink and swear. She accommodated them. The instruments started playing "Take another little piece of my heart now, baby." The audience went ballistic. They pressed forward to the stage even more. I cringed. Joplin had the audience in the palm of her hand. The house was rockin.' She didn't even have to sing—it was impossible to hear anything. The entire arena audience was swaying in unison.

Charlie was in a panic. He had never seen an audience act this way before. He yelled in my ear, "I'm going to stop the show now!"

"Please, Charlie, don't," I pleaded. "This has to be her last song. It'll be over soon. They'll leave peacefully. We won't let her come back for an encore. We can turn the house lights on as soon as this number is over."

Janis's road manager came over to me. "Pat, are you crazy? Get these fuckin' guys off the fuckin' stage right now or I'm going to pull the show!"

It was difficult to plead my case because no one could hear—we were just shouting in each other's ears. The house lights went on. I could see my $25,000 profit going right down the drain.

Janis stopped singing and said, "What the fuck is going on?"

The crowd yelled and screamed even louder.

Charlie said to me, "Go up and tell her to tell everyone to take their seats or I'll stop the show."

I couldn't say that to Janis Joplin and she wouldn't say that to her audience. But I had to do *something* or Charlie *would* stop the show. I'd have to issue refunds to everyone. Instead of a $25,000 profit, I'd suffer a $50,000 loss.

Janis stopped singing and turned to look at her road manager and me. The crowd booed. She walked back to us and said to me, "What the fuck is going on? If you want me to finish the fuckin' show, turn these fuckin' lights off."

Sergeant Patterson and Charlie came over to me. Janis and her road manager walked away. Jim said, "Charlie wants you to talk to this crowd and tell them the show can't go on until everyone is back in their seats. They have to move away from the front of the stage—it's too dangerous. Those kids up against the stage could get crushed to death."

"For Christ's sake, Jim, this isn't elementary school. If I go out and tell them that, they're going to laugh at me. They won't listen," I shouted.

"Well, either you establish some order or Charlie will stop the show. He wants me to call in dogs and more men."

"I'll do something," I said.

As I headed toward the mic, I saw Janis behind the amps. I walked up to her and said, "They want me to talk to the crowd about getting back in their seats. Those kids up against the stage barrier are getting crushed. It's dangerous. Could you help me out here? You could do one or two more numbers and end the show. They'll listen to you. I'm going to ask the audience to be cool so we can get the show going again. Is that okay with you?"

"Whatever." I was surprised when she added, "Go ahead and make your announcement, but don't ask me to tell them to sit down. You get that guy off this stage or I'm getting off." I was relieved she seemed to understand that I had to do something.

I walked up to the mic as the crowd was still booing. I said, "If you'll get back to your seats, we'll start the show again." They booed. I said, "Look, Janis wants to finish the concert. Please just back away from the stage. We don't want anyone to get crushed or hurt. Move back so we can start the show." Some people tried to move back but couldn't because the kids behind them couldn't or wouldn't move.

They started yelling in unison, "We want Janis!"

Janis to the Rescue

Janis took the mic out of my hand. The crowd started to cheer. She said, "He's The Man. He wants you to back off the stage and clear the aisles so we can start the show, okay?"

She was making me out to be the bad guy, which was all right with me. She repeated, "Back away from the stage just a little." When she said it, they listened. She turned around and nodded to the band, and they started into "Piece of My Heart."

The crowd went berserk. I thought, *only a few more minutes and it will all be over.*

I walked to the back of the stage and screamed above Janis's vocals to Charlie and Sergeant Patterson, "Turn the lights off and let her finish the show. She only has a few numbers left to do."

I didn't really know how many numbers she would do, but by now Charlie was getting used to the screaming.

The crowd kept waving their matches and lighters for more encores. She came back once, did another number, and left. I went up onstage and yelled that she had left the building. I didn't really know where she was, but we didn't want her doing any more songs. We wanted the people to leave. The house lights came up. I kept repeating that the show was over and thanked the audience for coming.

The show was over.

As the crowd was leaving the Arena I thought, *why am I in this business? It's too crazy, too stressful.* I walked back into the box office to see John Woods and finish my accounting business. He handed me a statement and said, "Sign here, Pat. Here's your check. It was a good night. You can bring Janis back anytime."

I looked at the statement. I had netted $15,000—more than three times what I'd made on The Beatles. It wasn't the $25,000 that I needed so badly, but I was back in business. I was happy.

I allocated that money to my accountant, Alma, to pay down my debt. She convinced my creditors to cut a hundred grand I owed down to $50,000. If I could land two or three more shows like this, I could pay them off. I would never again take a risk like buying the Electric Theater or Rock Falls Park again. I would never again dream too big and put myself in this position.

With fleeting regret, I thought of my mother and how she always wanted me to be a schoolteacher. No risks and no debt seemed like a great idea. Then I remembered—teachers earn less than $4,000 a year. I had just made nearly four years of a teacher's salary in one night. Maybe I'd stick it out a little longer.

I Wish I Had Your Life

As I stood on the stage that night, watching the crowd leave, I saw the 2,000 portable chairs on the arena floor were upside down, bent, or mangled.

Charlie came over to me and said, "If your insurance for tonight's show doesn't cover the cost of replacing those chairs, you'll have to buy us new ones."

"Don't worry, Charlie, I will," I assured him. I wondered how much one of those chairs cost. I could see my profits dwindling, but I had to do right by Charlie. I had the exclusive right to do all live performances at the arena. I needed him to have confidence in me and my ability to produce shows that were good for his building. He respected my judgment, and I wasn't going to let him down.

It took hundreds of employees to stage an event. I knew most of them by name. The janitors came in after the concert and worked all night to get the arena ready for the next event, which might be tomorrow. A different crew would come in early in the morning to set up. They would work right up to show time and then go home. If the next event was basketball, all the chairs and the stage would have to be removed and stored, and the basketball floor would have to be installed over the ice. The preparation for the different events was overwhelming.

As I trudged toward my car, I saw one of the arena employees punching in for his night's work. It was Gino, a janitor who lived in Level Green, near Trafford.

I said, "Hi, Gino. How's the family?"

He gave me a big smile and glanced at my briefcase. "I wish I had your life, Pat. You're leaving with all the cash and no worries. My workday's just starting. You wanna trade?"

I thought about that. "Yeah, Gino, sometimes I think I would. Especially tonight."

Chapter Four
Starting Out, 1956-1957

As I was about to graduate from Trafford High School in May 1956 and still working the Holiday House, I informed Johnny Bertera I was thinking the unthinkable. I wanted to quit.

"Why?" he asked.

"I want to go to college."

"What will you study?"

"I don't know. My mother wants me to be a schoolteacher."

"You know we have the hotel here and our manager Mr. Peoples needs some help. Would you be interested in going to Penn State for hotel management? When you graduate maybe you could work here and run the hotel. Who knows, maybe you could manage the whole operation someday."

I could learn how to manage the hotel? I'd never thought of that.

After considering my options and learning I would first have to study for two years at a state college I settled on Edinboro State Teachers College, close to home. My brother Mike had already broken the ice there for our family and had been attending Edinboro for the past two years. With his help, I was able to take my first classes in the summer of 1956. I did well in class, but when the summer session ended I had no money left to continue. I had to interrupt my college career and find another job. I applied at Westinghouse, the railroad, and the steel mill. But the very idea of working in any of those places, especially the steel mill, was depressing.

Westinghouse

Depressing or not, I landed a job and started working at Westinghouse, like everyone else in Trafford. But because I had taken college classes, I was offered one of their better jobs in the engineering department. Starting out as a drafting trainee—a white-collar job— I also took evening classes at Carnegie Tech, which were paid for by Westinghouse.

My father had worked at Westinghouse most of his life, sawing lumber on a table saw and building wooden crates to transport the generators. One winter day he went outside the S building where he worked to select lumber for a crate. He didn't notice that the bottom side of the wood piece he chose to cut was coated with ice. When he placed the frozen board on his table saw, it flew off the table top into the spinning blade, still in his hand, and the blade cut his thumb off. We felt sorry for him and Mum sobbed, but Dad was proud of it! He showed us a company form entitling him to $300 compensation for the loss of his thumb. That was the most money we'd ever seen in our home at one time.

Dad was also proud that I working in the N Building in a shirt and tie in an office that must have had 300 desks lined up in a series of rows. That office took up the entire Fourth floor. It was huge, but I felt like a caged animal there. It was not at all like the Holiday House.

I became friends with several of the employees who had been working there for years. Most of them hated their jobs. They were always hitting me up for quarters until payday for cigarettes, donuts, and coffee. These guys had been working there for years but they were always broke. That bothered me. I asked one of the older guys, "If you hate it here so much and you never have any money why do you still work here?"

He moaned, "I'm forty years old and I have three kids. Where would I work if I left? If I keep working here I'll have a pension when I retire in twenty-five years."

It's like being in prison, I thought to myself, *I'm only 18. Do I have to work here for 47 more years? I've only been here a few weeks and I hate it already. I can't do this for 47 more years.*

These guys were wishing their lives away. They were trapped in jobs they hated. I wanted more. I wanted a job like I had at the Holiday House, where I couldn't wait to go to work. I wanted to quit, but I knew that would be devastating to Mum and Dad and the last thing I wanted to do was hurt them.

Writing Songs

I started to write songs at home at night while I was working at Westinghouse. I wanted to form a singing group, but this time, instead of playing old standards and polkas like I did when I played bass with my Uncle Joe. I wanted a singing group that would perform original music geared towards teenagers. I was amazed at how fast I could write. The lyrics weren't great but I knew that kids my age would relate to them.

I teamed up with my buddy Dunch Bray to form a vocal group we called The Penn Boys because we were from Pennsylvania. How brilliant! Most of the singing groups at that time named themselves after cars or birds. All the good cars and birds were already taken, but nobody was naming themselves after their states, so that's what we did.

We rehearsed at the Italian Club, which my Dad ran for most of my younger years. Dad would often take me with him to the club on Sunday mornings after church for breakfast. I was ten years old and I loved it because dad would let me sweep up and I'd find nickels on the floor. God, I loved the smell of stale beer in that place. It was especially exciting for me whenever the Volpe brothers came in to empty the three slot machines. When they opened the machines to get the coins, they would always call me over and give me a handful of nickels and rack up a slew of free plays.

The Penn Boys consisted of lead singer and front man, Dunch Bray, Paul Mediate singing bass, and Emanuel "Cue

Ball" Krupar, who had such a great range that he could sing bass as well as falsetto. I became the fourth member and sang whatever part was needed at the time.

Because I had a sinus and allergy problem I didn't think I had a good singing voice. So although I understood harmony and had written the songs for the group, I replaced myself with Wayne Walthour.

On Saturday nights The Penn Boys and I would go to the Boosters dance in East Pittsburgh or to Pete Tambellini's dance at Burke Glen ballroom in Monroeville. We were more eager to see the live performers than meet or dance with the girls. Seeing live recording groups stimulated us and made us more determined to become successful.

After six long, painful months, I left my job at Westinghouse to concentrate on the record business. It was a monumental decision and quite emotional for my family. I felt I let them down. I had no real plans for my future. Fortunately, I still lived at home and had practically no expenses. After I left Westinghouse, I did nothing for about a month—I felt like a failure. I sunk to one of the lowest points in my life and became depressed. However, while working there I had saved $600, which, to me, was an enormous amount of money.

Your Cleaners

My oldest brother JuJu had quit his job with Wall Avenue Cleaners and opened a small dry cleaning business in nearby Level Green called Your Cleaners. Learning I saved $600, he suggested I use it to buy into one half of the business, which I did. He planned on expanding our new enterprise by purchasing used tuxedos and renting them out mainly for high school proms.

My job was to drive our panel truck through the nearby towns, knock on doors, and ask people if they needed dry cleaning services. If they said yes, I would take their clothes to our shop. Returning every evening with a truckload of soiled clothes, we would dry clean and press everything. We charged a quarter to launder a shirt, a dollar to clean and press a suit and fifty cents for pants and that included pickup and delivery.

I also visited area high schools during prom season to rent our tuxedos for twenty-five bucks. JuJu found a supplier who sold us hundreds of used tuxedoes for $600 just in time for the upcoming prom season. Our friend Tony Berardo—a good looking, popular high school student at North Huntingdon—became our salesman. He convinced so many students at the schools to rent our tuxedos that we recouped our investment in one prom season.

After a few months of working day and night seven days a week and not getting paid, I came to hate the dry cleaning business almost as much as Westinghouse. It just wasn't for me. My brother had a wife and 2 kids and was having a hard time making ends meet. I wanted to help him, but my heart wasn't in it, so I asked him if he would mind if I left.

The Del Vikings

My cousin, Pooner Venturo, found out that John Koloney, who lived in nearby Trafford Terrace, had a reel-to-reel tape recorder and recorded four of my songs.

We listened to the tapes constantly and we loaned them to anyone who asked. The next week we attended the Boosters Dance Hall in East Pittsburgh. It was the biggest dance in the Pittsburgh area, mainly because of Jay Michael, the number one disc jockey in town on WCAE radio.

I gave Jay a copy of the tape and asked him to listen to our group. A few days later, he called and said he had made arrangements with a New York record producer to come to the WCAE studio at the Carlton House in Pittsburgh to audition several groups including The Penn Boys. The date was set for next month. We anxiously waited for that audition and practiced every day. We kept telling the whole town (and ourselves) "this is it, we're going big time."

On the day of the audition we drove to Pittsburgh, which was a challenge because none of us knew how to get there! Somehow we found our way to the lobby of the Carlton House. But when the elevator operator, a black guy dressed in a maroon uniform, said "Floor?" we didn't know what he meant. We had never been in an elevator before. Again he asked, "Which floor do you want?"

"Which floor do we want?"

"Yeah, where do you want to go? Oh never mind. You're here for the WCAE audition, right?"

I wondered, *how would he know that?* We must have looked like real country hicks, but we were too excited and too naïve to feel embarrassed.

I didn't know it, but the Carlton House was where all music business people—record companies, promoters, songwriters, and producers—were located. It was the Mecca of the recording industry in Pittsburgh. We entered the WCAE reception area to be greeted by the most beautiful creature we had ever seen—a tall, statuesque blonde who took our name and checked us off her list. Escorting us to a waiting area, she offered refreshments and told us to wait until our name was called.

There must have been 50 other hopefuls waiting for their audition. Most of them were black groups dressed to the nines. My brother JuJu gave us white dinner jackets with everything to match as though we were going to the prom. But our competition blew us away. We realized before we even heard them sing we were no match for the black groups. We were early for our appointed time, but we didn't mind waiting. It was fun and interesting to hear the black artists talk in a musical language we had never heard before. We'd had no contact with any black groups and very few black people lived in Trafford. But these guys were great singers with great original material

It was our turn to audition. As we entered the studio we were introduced to an impeccably dressed gentleman who was the producer. We had never seen a New York record producer before. "Okay guys, I don't have a lot of time and there are a lot of groups out there who want to be heard. I want you to sing your two best songs, the songs you think could be hits. I want to see your stage presence. Sing like you're onstage in front of an audience. Understand?"

This is it, I thought. *This is our big chance.* All our dreams could come true at this very moment—recording contracts, hit records, national tours. But when our bass singer, Paul Mediate, started us off he was flat. We were off-key. "Stop" said the producer, "I know you guys are nervous. Try it again. Let's go. I'm in a hurry."

Again we sounded hopelessly flat. We blew it. The producer's parting words were "Don't call us we'll call you."

It was disappointing, but to have been in a Pittsburgh radio station and with a New York record producer was exciting. We were more determined than ever to become recording stars.

Our friend Jay Michael was sympathetic. "I know a record producer who handles The Del Vikings and he has a record label. His name is Joe Averbach. I'll line up an audition for you.

The Del Vikings—a group of Air Force servicemen stationed at the 911 Air Wing base at the Greater Pittsburgh Airport—had just scored a major hit with "Come Go with Me."

The group approached Pittsburgh disc jockey Barry Kaye in 1956 for help. Barry auditioned and recorded the Del Vikings in the basement of his home and then sent the tape to Joe Averbach, the owner of a Pittsburgh-based record distributorship called R B & S (which stood for Rhythm, Blues and Spirituals). Averbach added instrumental backing to Barry's a-cappella recordings in a downtown hotel room studio with a few of the Del Viking's Air Force buddies and released the recordings on his own record label with "Come Go with Me" as the B side. B-sides were generally ignored, but when DJ's started playing "Come Go with Me" as the A-side it got an instant reaction. Their listeners loved it. Sensing a major hit in the works, Joe contacted Randy Wood at Dot Records for national distribution and suddenly Joe's little local record company (named Fee Bee Records after his wife) was a national success.

"Come Go with Me" —originally recorded in Barry Kaye's basement—went on to become a million seller, a classic perennial hit. When the Del Vikings' second record, "Whispering Bells," also hit the top of the charts it made Joe Averbach a big deal in the record business.

Knowing Joe was searching for more hit acts to produce, Jay Michael set up an appointment for me. I played the tape my group had recorded in John Koloney's basement. "I like your songs," Joe said, "but I don't like your singing group. Would you let me have your songs for the Del Vikings?"

I didn't know what to think. I wanted The Penn Boys to sing my songs. I didn't want to give them to another group. But The Del Vikings were one of the hottest acts in the country and I liked them.

The Penn Boys were anxious to hear what Joe had to say about our tape. When I told them what Joe wanted they said "Do it. Don't hold yourself back for us. You can always write more songs for The Penn Boys."

So I agreed to let the Del Vikings record my music. In the fall of 1957, they released two of my songs, "I'm Spinning" backed with "You Say You Love Me."

I started hanging out with the group. They invited me to a dance they were headlining at Market Square in Pittsburgh and I took my co-writer Dunch with me. We didn't realize it was an all-black event until we got there. We were the only two white guys in the place. But The Del Vikings made us feel special. Everybody at the show treated us like stars. This was my first taste of what it was like to be a 'behind the scenes" person in the entertainment business and I liked it.

Unfortunately, just before "I'm Spinning" was released, an internal conflict resulted in The Del Vikings dividing into two groups with the same name. "I'm Spinning" was released by Krip Johnson and the Dell Vikings (with two L's) on Dot

Records, while the Del Vikings (with one L) released a different recording on Mercury Records. So there were two Del Vikings records out at the same time. "I'm Spinning" sold well, but it would have done much better if it had been the only Del Vikings release.

Everyone in town thought I got rich from The Dell Vikings recording. In reality, I received almost no royalties from it. But I didn't care. That record gave me the recognition I needed to get established in the music business. The jocks would mention my name every time they played the record. I figured that was payment enough. It made me a big deal.

When Dot Records took over "I'm Spinning" on Joe's Fee Bee label and distributed the record nationally. I felt I had made it big.

I continued to perform and record with The Penn Boys for another year or so, working with notable recording artists like The Diamonds, who had a monster 1957 hit single with "Little Darlin."

I would continue to carry with me the lessons I learned during this period of my life throughout my career. I look back on those days with great fondness and gratitude for the doors it opened and the opportunities The Penn Boys gave me.

Chapter Five
Sold Out in 1970

Three Dog Night, February 6, 1970

In the late summer of 1969 Tim Tormey called to ask what I thought of a new group hitting it big in L.A. They were playing regularly at a club on Sunset Boulevard, not too far from Dick Clark's office. Dick always kept up with the times and the new bands. He would even disguise himself sometimes and hang out at Venice Beach just to see what the hippies were up to.

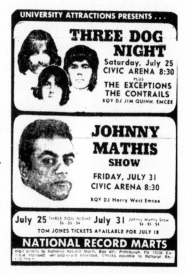

Dick was interested in a group called Three Dog Night. The group had a big hit with "One" and Dick wanted to see the act to determine if it was worthy to headline one of his national tours. Staging multiple dates and tours in many different cities made Dick appear even bigger than he actually was. But make no mistake about it—Dick Clark was a major influence. With acts like Three Dog Night he was trying to get away from his "teenie bopper" image. He could see a major shift coming as more radio listeners began tuning in to the new FM music and he wanted in on it.

Dick wanted to make sure Three Dog Night could sell out arenas. Listening to their first album he heard multiple hits.

"Eli's Coming," "Easy to Be Hard" and *"Celebrate"* were all great songs. Dick was right about them. We booked the band far in advance, before most other promoters caught on. We knew Three Dog Night would be giants.

My arrangement with Dick Clark had me dealing with Tim again. That was great. Tim had Dick take care of the required fifty percent deposit when the act was booked, with the balance due just before the performance. Dick didn't mind paying the advance deposit to the act, but Tim did. Because of Dick's huge reputation, Tim often convinced the agents to waive the fifty percent deposit. I never had to put up the deposits either, especially if I knew the act or the agent. That was a big advantage for me because I could book multiple shows without upfront money.

By the time Three Dog Night played Pittsburgh their album had soared to the top of the charts. They were the hottest act in the country. We priced tickets at $4, $5 and $6 and sold out immediately. I was on a roll. At this rate, I figured, I would be able to satisfy all of my debts from the Electric Theatre disaster quickly.

The night of the concert I heard all the usual unpleasant comments from the arena workers. They had still not adjusted to the cultural changes in the business. You could smell pot throughout the venue and see the audience passing joints.

One of our lady ushers shook her finger at me. "Look at that. It's disgraceful. This is going to be just like that Janis girl." Dressed up in her long black skirt and frilly white-lace blouse she looked like she was ushering an opera. *Why doesn't the arena have a different set of ushers and workers for the rock shows?* I wondered. *We need college students.*

I walked on with my eyes on the floor so I didn't have to see anyone. The box office was my favorite place to be during a concert. Usually it was only John Woods (the box office manager} and me. That is where I escaped the arena employees, who hated rock concerts, and the more persistent customers who couldn't understand why they weren't being seated close to the stage. They would complain, "I guess you have to know somebody to get good tickets." People thought I held back the good seats for my favored friends. But I never gave that a thought. My only concern was selling tickets and getting out of debt. I didn't care who bought them. Oh, what I would have given for an arena with 10,000 front row seats!

I liked being in the box office for the peace and solace and the brief respite it gave me from dealing with the artists. I didn't particularly like dealing with stars. Some were demanding, difficult and greedy. Yes, I liked their music and I wanted to give the audience a great show, but that didn't mean that I had to fraternize with the acts. It was strictly business.

I developed a sterling reputation for integrity with artists, managers and agents. Often, the act didn't come to me to get paid until the show was over. In later years, when we promoted Bruce Springsteen at Three Rivers Stadium, the tour manager simply called me at the box office and said, "Just send our check to Premier Talent." Bruce Springsteen trusted us enough to mail a check for $750,000 to him. Believe me, he got his money.

At the time of the Three Dog Night show the transition from AM radio to FM radio was still not complete. AM radio was still a powerhouse. So I had Pittsburgh's KQV-AM station present the show. Three Dog Night was not thrilled about it. Acts like theirs and Tommy James and The Shondells of "Hanky Panky" fame were trying to break away from bubble gum and teeny bopper labels. They were trying to write and record music that would appeal to FM listeners. In Tommy's case, the result was their big hit, "Crimson and Clover."

As the show began. people were still pushing through the turnstiles and rushing to their seats. Some patrons tried barging through the seating directors only to be turned back by Sgt. Bill Evans, a husky part-time security guard on the arena staff. "It's going to be another tough night, Pat," he moaned, "Just like the

Janis Joplin show. Tell me the truth now, Pat. Should I tell my guys to get ready for another tough night?"

"No, Bill. I don't think we're going to have any problems tonight."

A rock concert at the Arena was still a relatively new phenomenon and the employees still had not accepted the cultural changes. At this time, the agents would let me select an opening act for the show and I usually added one of the groups that I was managing as the opener. Nobody really paid much attention to the opening act and latecomers could disturb the audience without irritating anyone, so it worked out well for everyone…except the opening act. Opening a show was not the big break into stardom they hoped for.

I would walk out of the box-office to watch the openers as promised and I was expected to be in their dressing room after they got off the stage to offer them my critical analysis of the performance. I wanted to be tactful and optimistic but I was known for not going easy on anyone who asked for my advice.

As I was listening to the opening act I looked around at all 16,000 seats in the cavernous dome and I could feel the tension and smell the smoke filling the arena. The crowd was getting restless, eager for the real show to begin, ready for the stars of the show. I began my long walk around the arena to the back of the stage. I walked into the opening act's dressing room to psyche them up a little and told them what I thought they wanted to hear. After their performance, with the twenty-minute intermission over, I walked on stage in my normal attire of jeans, brown Dingo western boots, brown leather jacket down to my waist, and aviator sunglasses.

Because KQV radio was presenting the show, I let Chuck Brinkman emcee it. I hoped they wouldn't be too corny and just announce the show without wasting time or boring the audience. From the rear corner of the stage I could see Three Dog Night standing at the top of the back stage steps. I flashed a signal to Chuck at the microphone indicating that the act was ready. It was time to announce "And now let's have a big KQV welcome for THREE DOG NIGHT!"

It was the same as it was with Janice, the crowd reacting with a wild ovation as Three Dog Night walked on stage. The audience welcomed them by immediately rushing towards the front of the stage. As the band played its first number the crowd stood in amazement and appreciation. It was like they had never attended a concert and didn't know what to expect. When they started playing their hit, "Celebrate," the audience went crazy and pushed closer to the stage. The music was blaring and the arena was filled with the sweet smell of marijuana. I was watching all of this from stage right. Charlie Strong, the arena manager, came up to me on stage and yelled into my ear, "Aren't you going to do anything?"

"Like what?" I yelled back over the deafening sound.

"I'm going to stop the show. This is getting too far out of hand. You have to go on stage and get these kids in their seats," Charlie shouted.

It felt like he was punishing me, as if I was responsible for the behavior of my audience. To Charlie, I was the cause of the problem. It was my act, my show, and I had to do whatever it took to settle the crowd.

I had difficulty understanding what the problem really was until Charlie pointed to the police at the side of the stage. I saw they were ready for a riot.

"Either you go out to that microphone and get those kids settled down or I'm going to turn on all the lights and turn the sound off and stop the show."

"Charlie, you can't do that."

"This is my arena. Either you do what I tell you or I will nod to John Moriarity over there and he will carry out my orders. The police will come on the stage and this show will be over."

I couldn't believe it. It was the Janis Joplin show all over again. *Was it always going to be like this,* I wondered as I walked up to Cory Wells who was singing at the microphone.

He looked startled. My lips were almost touching his ear as I shouted "I'm having a problem with the arena management. We have to stop." The other singers, Danny Hutton and Chuck Negron, looked at Cory and me and they all stopped singing right in the middle of "Celebrate."

The four of us had a huddle right there on the stage. I explained the arena management wanted to end the show unless we got the kids back in their seats. I pleaded with them, "Tell the audience to move back and get in their seats so we can start the show again."

"No. We can't do that. That's not good for our image. We want them to enjoy our show. They are into this. It's one of our best audiences. So what if they're standing?"

"I agree. But it's not me. It's the police and the arena. We're going to have to do something." I said.

"You mean *you're* going to have to do something," Danny yelled.

"Look Danny, let's you and me go up to the microphone and talk to the audience. I'll tell them to sit down and you can say anything you'd like, but I'll do the dirty work. Okay?"

"Okay, let's do it."

I motioned to Charlie I wanted to talk to the audience and needed the sound back on. Charlie gave the signal. I heard a bang and a humming sound and realized the microphone was turned back on. I stood there for what seemed like an eternity and wondered what I was going to say. I liked wearing the aviator sunglasses because nobody could see my eyes. It was a buffer between the audience and me.

I approached the microphone, "Okay. If you want this show to continue, listen up." The audience started booing. I glanced over at Charlie and saw the police by his side. The audience saw them, too.

Danny Hutton walked up to my side and took my microphone. Pointing to me he said, "He's the man and the man says that we can't continue unless you back away from the stage." The booing got even louder. I was the "man." I was the bad guy. But if that's what it took to get the show going again, it was alright with me. I would be the man.

The crowd started backing away from the stage. I walked over to Charlie and the police and said, "I think it will be alright until they finish." The show went on.

It took a long time for management to realize rock concerts were not basketball games or the Civic Light Opera. Ultimately, though, the bottom line was that rock concerts were profitable. When both the Civic Light Opera and the professional basketball team abandoned the arena and the older ushers quit, management started hiring younger people. Charlie saw the light. He proposed to Tim and me that we bring in a summer concert series to replace the Civic Light Opera.

My concert business was about to go into high gear.

Led Zeppelin: The Night Pittsburgh Sold Out of Dom Perignon

The English acts were always difficult to deal with. I used to laugh to myself and think they were all still upset over The Boston Tea Party. On March 30, 1970, I played Led Zeppelin at the Civic Arena. The date sold out in advance as expected. One of the rider requirements in the group's contract was going to  become a problem; it called for me to provide two cases of Dom Perignon Champagne for their dressing room.

I was lucky to get this date, thanks to my good friend, Jack Hooke, who was friends with Zeppelin's manager, Peter Grant. The way the concert business works is that the local promoter in each town gets a call from an agent asking for availabilities for certain time periods. This might be as far as 6 months in advance, but that was not the case in this situation. Everyone wanted Led Zeppelin to play their town. I was lucky Jack could influence the act to play Pittsburgh, that the Civic Arena was available, and that the date made routing sense for the band.

For this show, Led Zeppelin had an extensive rider. This was a new trend with major acts. Every contract included a "rider," which is an extension of the contract. In the 50s and early 60s it was just a one page agreement—essentially, "who, what, when, where and why." In the late 60s, though, major acts started adding certain requirements to the one page agreement.

It started with requests for spotlights or additions to the sound systems. Back when Tim Tormey and I promoted The Beatles in 1964 they used the same Civic Arena sound system that was used to announce basketball games. The Beatles showed up with all their equipment in a Ford Econoline van. And there was no rider.

Later, artists started requesting supplemental sound systems. Then it was special food and beverages to be provided for their road crew. Food demands got more complex. In the old days promoters would provide all the acts with Kentucky Fried Chicken because it was cheap and easy. KFC became so common that the acts started writing "absolutely NO Kentucky Fried Chicken" into their riders. Before long, riders grew from one page to over twenty pages.

Acts began to request more complicated equipment as well. Instead of wanting just a piano, they might demand a 9-foot Steinway grand piano or a Hammond B3 organ with two Leslie speakers. Pianos and organs were big and bulky. More stagehands were required to handle the additional equipment, which increased costs. The potential for disagreements grew. Acts were trying to outdo each other with their requests and the size of their riders.

In addition to the supplemental sound system, Led Zeppelin wanted catering and made a myriad of other unnecessary demands. They wanted their dressing rooms stocked with two cases of Dom Perignon, the most expensive champagne you could buy.

I usually didn't bother sending my runner out to buy the liquor until the last minute. If I bought the liquor ahead of time, I would have to keep it in my office and hope nobody stole it or drank it. Jimmy "Chuncie" Vaccaro was my assistant. His job was to supply everything the act requested in the dressing room rider.

On the day before the concert, he went to the liquor store to buy the champagne and the liquor the band required. After going to several liquor stores with no success, he called me and said, "I have a problem, I can't find two cases of Dom Perignon Champagne anywhere in the city. Can't we just give them any champagne? What's the difference? Champagne is champagne. Let's just give them what I can get."

"No, this is a big act. They're going to be like The Beatles. We have to get the Dom Perignon. Did you try Horne's department store downtown?"

"Horne's Department Store sells liquor?"

"Yes." They had a liquor store on the first floor and at the time it was the best place in Pittsburgh to buy high-end liquor. Jimmy asked the clerk for 24 bottles of Dom Perignon. The clerk impatiently explained that, "You will not find two cases of Dom Perignon in the entire city of Pittsburgh. You must order that item well in advance. Nobody stocks that much Dom. But you can have all the Dom we've got—which is 3 bottles. You want me to order them?" He spoke in a condescending manner as though we should have known better.

"No, I need it tonight."

"Well you won't be able to find that much anywhere in the city. If I don't have it, nobody else will have it either. But I do have other champagne that's good. It's about the same price close to $100 a bottle," the clerk said rather proudly.

I should have called the band's manager Peter Grant and explained my dilemma, but I knew he would think that I just didn't want to pay for the expensive champagne. Besides, Peter

Grant had a vicious reputation—he hated concert promoters because he thought we were making all the money. I told Jimmy to go back to Horne's to buy the three bottles of Dom and 21 bottles of the second best champagne for $100 a bottle, which I thought was outrageous, but I figured "what's the difference?" We didn't think about it after that. We were happy we got the equipment on the stage on time, which we thought was more important than the champagne.

On the night of the show, the caterer had the food and beverages set up for the roadies backstage. Another caterer had a set up in each of the band members' dressing rooms. Jimmy Vaccaro put the two cases of the expensive champagne substitute in the specified dressing room.

Dressing rooms were always a problem at the Arena. I had converted the hockey locker room into a "star" dressing room. It didn't always go over well with the more temperamental acts. Sometimes I would rent carpet to cover the cement floor and pipes and drapes to cover the block walls and rent luxury living room furniture to make the locker room feel more like home.

Jimmy, as instructed in the rider, left the champagne in the star's dressing room. Zeppelin could quickly see by looking at the box that they were not getting Dom. I was in our box office and usually stayed there during the show just to stay away from temperamental artists. Showtime is a bad time to be around artists because they're usually nervous and they all have some degree of stage fright. I got a call from the road manager who said, "Pat, could you come down to the dressing room?"

From the sound of his voice, I knew this was trouble. Road managers almost never want to see you before the show. They stay away from you because they think you're going to introduce them to someone for an autograph or a picture. I hurried to other side of the arena and knocked on the dressing room door. The road manager pointed angrily towards the two cases and grabbed a bottle of the expensive champagne out of the box, held it up to my face and said, "What the fuck is this? Is this fuckin' Dom Perignon? No! Can you fuckin' read?"

Crash! He threw the $100 bottle of champagne against the concrete wall. It broke and the champagne burst out all over me and ran over the floor. I stood there in amazement and shock. *This guy is either insane or high on something,* I thought. Then he grabbed another bottle and says, "Is this fuckin' Dom? No!" He slams that bottle against the wall and again it splashes all over me. He repeated this over and over again until all 24 bottles were smashed against the wall. $2,500 worth of champagne disappeared before my eyes.

When he was finished humiliating me, I tried to explain. "You're in Pittsburgh, PA. We couldn't get 24 bottles of Dom. None of the liquor stores could afford to stock that much inventory. There's very little demand for expensive champagne in Pittsburgh and it must be ordered. I'm sorry—I should have ordered it in advance."

I had learned years ago that dealing with a superstar ego is difficult for a promoter. It is even more of a challenge when you deal with stars under the influence of drugs and alcohol. I had been around many big name stars and was never in awe of any of them. I just wanted to play the date, have everything go well and get the show over with. I wasn't interested in autographs, pictures or bringing people back stage. When I had to deal with groups with this attitude I remembered to take my mother's advice, "Bite your tongue," and I did. I let the road manager have his way and didn't say a word.

We sold 12,331 tickets for a gross of $57,562. Another big winner!

The concert business helped my college agency business, University Attractions. All the student buyers wanted to come to Pittsburgh to see the major concerts. I made sure they never paid and had good seats. I arranged for them to go back stage. This paid off big for me when the buyers booked shows for their homecoming events. The concert business was doing well, and now I was raking it in with my agency business, which had no risk.

All I ever wanted, on the night of a show was for it to be the next day. The next morning I could think, *Oh, thank God that show is over.* In spite of the champagne issue, the Zeppelin show turned out to be successful and profitable for all of us. The audience loved it and apparently the lack of Dom did not affect the band's performance.

Later, I found out from one of the band's roadies the road manager was collecting two cases of Dom Perignon from every promoter in the US on that tour and they weren't even drinking it. The roadie was instructed to load the champagne on one of the trucks after the show for an exclusive party after the tour. The champagne had nothing to do with the concert.

Aerosmith: No Turkey Roll
(Three Rivers Stadium, June 12, 1976)

In the summer of 1976 the Boston band, Aerosmith, had built themselves into a stadium act with several major hits, embarked on a tour with ZZ Top. I played the double bill at Three Rivers Stadium on June 12. A stadium show was always a major event to produce. I looked forward to its challenges and learned you have to pay attention to every little detail.

Converting a stadium from a baseball field to a concert venue takes a lot of planning and work. The first problem is availability of a date. Even though a concert is usually a 3 to 4 hour event (this show would be double that), it takes at least 3 to 4 days to convert and reset a sports stadium to a concert facility. Usually, it takes one or two days before the show to set up and a day after the show and to tear down, load out, and remove the staging. Hundreds of employees are needed to work around the clock, consisting of IATSE stagehands, stadium grounds crew, teamsters, our own crew, and additional temporary help…just to convert the facility.

As many as 30 to 40 trailer trucks loaded with staging, sound, lights and band equipment required up to 20 unloaders and stagehands to unload the equipment from the truck to the tailgate and then a different group of union workers to move the equipment from the tailgate to the stage and finally to the actual location on the stage.

From the beginning, the show was fraught with problems. The fans with tickets showed up early. So did the fans that had no tickets but wanted in. Alcohol and drugs were plentiful. The restroom facilities were not conveniently placed or easily reached so some people didn't care where they relieved themselves. It was not a pleasant day to be the promoter.

During Aerosmith's set a patron found his way into the electric room and turned off the power to the stage. Obviously, this irritated the act who became more upset when they went into their Winnebago dressing room and discovered our caterer had made a mistake. When we received the rider of the contract, which specified the food and beverages the act wanted in their dressing room, it specifically stated "there shall be no turkey roll." Our caterer misinterpreted the request and thought it meant Aerosmith *wanted* turkey roll. He prominently placed the turkey roll on the banquet table in the Winnebago. When the group saw that they behaved the way immature acts with unlimited power often do—they destroyed the interior of the recreational vehicle. Catering was a big thing. As Tim Tormey said, "Today, the act judges you as a promoter not by the myriad of problems that you solve, but by what your caterer was like."

The concert began around 4:30 p.m. and ran well past midnight. 54,000 ticket holders paid $8.75 to see it. We paid the city about $45,000 in amusement tax, which was 10 percent of the gross. Mayor Pete Flaherty (who *always* gave me a hard time) later said that if there were going to be any more rock concerts at the stadium, they could not exceed seven hours, the gates had to open earlier, there had to be more portable toilets, and those under the influence of alcohol or drugs would be refused admission.

David Krebs and Steve Lieber, the managers of Aerosmith, complained that since we obviously were not concerned about their act's request for no turkey roll we should not expect Aerosmith to ever perform for us again.

Our next concert on July 24, 1976 featured The Eagles and Fleetwood Mac. The crowd was mild in comparison to Aerosmith and ZZ Top, but at one point in the concert even this crowd began to get disruptive. The Eagles stopped the music and one of the members pleaded with the crowd, "You've already had one bad concert here at this stadium this summer. Let's not have another one." The show played without any further incident.

Chicago (August 14, 1970, and November 11, 1970)

Abby Hoffer was one of my favorite agents. I believed and trusted him. He called me one day and said, "Pat, I've got a new act that's going to be big and I need a date at the arena. I had a date fall out. You'd be doing me a big favor if you booked them for me."

"Who's the act?"

"Chicago Transit Authority. They have a brass section and a great sound and by the time they get to your date in Pittsburgh they will have the number one record in the country. I guarantee it."

"How much?"

"Ten grand."

"Ten grand and they're not even known yet! You're crazy."

"Maybe not in Pittsburgh, but they are selling out everywhere they play and I'm telling you if you do me this favor, I won't forget it."

"I have Blood Sweat and Tears booked and I think they will do really well. Your act sounds like they could be similar with all those horns. I don't want to take a chance with an unknown act. Blood Sweat and Tears is the act I should go with," I told him, "I can't have all that competition close together."

"The Chicago Transit Authority is a better act, Pat, you'll see."

I caved in. "Okay, Abby, only for you." This was the way our business ran. Sometimes you had to do things you didn't want to.

On August 14, 1970 Chicago performed to a completely sold out Civic Arena. A total of 12,952 tickets for a gross of $58,439, were sold. I could have played another show—the demand was so great. Not only did I have to tell Abby he was right, but I had to beg for another date.

On November 11 that same year, I booked another show with Chicago. I had never booked the same act twice in the same year before, but they sold out again—12, 917 tickets for a gross of $58, 262. Blood Sweat and Tears, on the other hand, only did about 66% capacity. I never booked them again. But I did book Chicago ten more times. I never ever doubted Abby again and I have to admit, Chicago became one of my favorite acts and they were always a pleasure to play. The audience actually sat in their seats during the show!

PAT DiCESARE PRESENTS

JETHRO TULL

plus

MOUNTAIN

CIVIC ARENA 8:30

FRIDAY OCTOBER 30

KQV D. J. JAY DAVIS, EMCEE

CHICAGO

plus

★ STILLWATER ★ SEALS AND CROFTS

CIVIC ARENA 8:30

WEDNESDAY NOV. 11

KQV D. J. JIM QUINN, EMCEE

OCT. 30 JETHRO TULL $6-$5-$4 NOV. 11 CHICAGO $6-$5-$4

TICKETS AT CIVIC ARENA AND ALL

NATIONAL RECORD MARTS

Chapter Six
Tim Tormey, 1957-1960

By 1957 I knew Joe Averback well enough to ask him to help me get a job in the record business. He told me he didn't have any jobs available at his record company or his record distributorship, but he knew someone who might need a stock boy. I didn't know it, but what was about to unfold would prove to be the biggest break of my life.

Being a stock boy wasn't really what I had in mind, but I figured I was breaking into "the business." The job consisted of sweeping the floors at night, stocking the records, pulling orders for the record stores and juke box operators, packing the records, and driving the packages to the bus station or the post office. It was just grunt work.

Nobody could believe I quit a great job at Westinghouse, with the promise of a great future, to take a low-end job as a stock boy. But I was eager to take *any* job in the record business and I considered it a stroke of great luck. Joe called my soon-to-be mentor for the rest of my life, Tim Tormey, and told him I was looking for any type of work in the record business I could get.

Tim told Joe, "Send him down to see me." His office was located on Fifth Avenue in the wholesale district in the uptown part of the city of Pittsburgh, often referred to as "Jew Town." Tim was a unique person. He was Irish and moved to Pittsburgh from New Rochelle, New York. He hired me and sent me to work across the street from his office at a place called Leslie

One-Stop. There I was to meet the manager, Jack Shook. The concept of a One Stop in the record business was to sell records primarily to jukebox operators and small "mom and pop" record stores. There were at least 500,000 jukeboxes on location in the United States. If you wanted a million-selling record you could sell half that to jukebox operators alone. My job was to concentrate on these operators to get them to buy our records.

The way the record business operated at this time was that each label had representation in every major market. If your record came out on RCA Victor, they would have a distributor in each major market: Pittsburgh, Baltimore, Philadelphia, Chicago, and so on. The same was true for Columbia, Mercury, Decca, and on down the line. All of the labels needed and wanted representation. There might have been 20 different distributors in Pittsburgh. A distributor usually represented more than one label, especially the independents, where there could be up to fifty different labels being represented by one distributor.

If you were a jukebox operator and you wanted to buy 10 new hits of the day you might have to drive to ten different distributors to pick up your records. Thus, the idea for a onestop record distributor was created. The one-stop would buy all the hits from any label and stock them all in one location for resale. A jukebox operator only had to drive to the one-stop to buy all the hits for only five cents more per record. A single

45 rpm record that retailed for ninety-nine cents wholesaled for sixty cents from the main distributor. If you bought the record from us at a one-stop, we added five cents to the price. This was our profit. We sold it to the jukebox operator or retailer for sixty-five cents for the convenience of being able to buy all the hits at one location. There was no longer a need to drive all over the city to ten different distributors.

I worked for Jack Shook, who managed The Leslie One-Stop for Tim Tormey. Tim was the manager of Record Distributors which was also located on Fifth Avenue across the street from Leslie One Stop. Both companies were owned by Lou Boorstien, who lived in New York City. This was my first real job in the record business. I was 18 years old and had only been to the city of Pittsburgh a couple of times in my life. That alone was very frightening, as I had no idea where anything was located in the city.

My job was to drive throughout the city to all the major labels and pick up the hits that Jack Shook ordered. I had never driven throughout the city before and it was quite scary. I didn't tell Jack that for fear of losing my job but I was constantly stopping to ask strangers for directions (GPS tracking systems were still 50 years in the future). Once I found myself in the Hill District, an all-black area of the city. I stopped at a gas station and walked into the shop where an older black mechanic was working on a car. "I'm lost," I told him. "Could you tell me how I could get to Fifth Avenue?"

"Boy, you *are* lost. This is Center Avenue. Keep driving down the hill and you'll see the city. But get your white ass out of here quick before your car gets stripped and you get in trouble and don't ever come to this part of town again." He said this in a kind way. I didn't understand what he meant. This was all foreign to me. I was naive about racial divisions, but I took his advice.

After picking up the records and returning to our office I placed them in bins at Leslie One-Stop. Jack asked me to help him behind the counter when jukebox operators came in to order new records for their jukeboxes and I liked that. Most of the operators came in to buy new records every other week.

The jukebox operators also dealt with cigarette machines, bowling machines, and the big money makers—poker and slot machines. To keep their good customers satisfied the jukebox operators kept the playlists on their jukeboxes current with the hits of the day. The operators complained they lost money on jukeboxes and the only reason they serviced their customer with jukeboxes was to get their bowling machine and cigarette machine business, as well as their high-profit gambling machine business. They were usually in a bad mood when dealing with us.

Gambling was illegal. The bar owners were very careful when paying off a hit in front of any stranger. The regular customers knew this. If a regular customer had a hit and there was a stranger in the bar the customer knew to wait until the stranger left. Then the bartender paid him off. But things didn't always go so well, like the time Greenie—an obese jukebox operator with a heavy dark beard and a dark complexion who often reminded me of Popeye's enemy Bluto—came in and told me, "I got arrested last night."

"You did?" I shouted in surprise. I had never known anyone who was arrested before. I wondered why he wasn't in jail, but I didn't say it out loud.

"Yeah, I was set up. This guy came in and played the machine and hit. He had been coming in for a while, many times. He hit a jackpot and wanted to cash-in and when I paid him he flipped out his badge and said, 'You're under arrest.'"

Some jukebox operators had as many as a 1,000 locations. We had to do special things for those guys. Anyone who could buy a thousand copies of one record was a VIP in the industry and he expected a good deal.

There were some strange characters who came in to buy records. Most of the operators were of Italian, Greek, or Jewish descent. Some were probably organized crime figures, but I was naïve about that, too.

One day, Tim sent his secretary, Mary, across the street to our One-Stop to tell me Tim wanted to see me in his office. That got me worried—I had not seen Tim Tormey since the day he hired me. But when I got there he said, "I understand you have a record that's getting some airplay. Tell me about it."

I told him my song had been released on Dot records by the Dell Vikings and it was on the Billboard charts. He was impressed and started taking a greater interest in me. Because my song went to the top of the charts in Pittsburgh I earned more respect not only from Tim, but from all of my fellow workers.

One day, after I had worked with Jack Shook for about a year, Tim Tormey sent for me. Tim always had a cigarette in his mouth and he had a strange way of smoking it that fascinated me. When he took cigarette out of his mouth, instead of putting it in an ashtray, he would put it up on one end and let the filter part of the cigarette sit in an upright position. I was mesmerized by that. When I talked to him I watched the cigarette smoke curling up towards his eyes. He would move his head slightly to the side to get the smoke away and then take another drag and put it back on his desk resting perpendicular on its filtered end, not at all like anyone else who smoked. I was amazed he never used the ash tray while smoking. With the cigarette smoke still curling around his face, he said to me, "From now on, you will work for me at Record Distributors. You will do the same type of work here that you did for Jack."

He was a short, rugged guy who spoke with authority. He was smart and he commanded respect. He was a tough negotiator, but he was fair and honest. I felt honored to have been invited to work for him. Soon he came to regard me as his assistant. He seemed to favor me. My fellow workers at Record Distributors soon started giving me a hard time because I was, in their words, "Tim's boy."

"Buy Yourself a Suit."

After I had been with Tim for about six months, he called me in his office and said, "Do you own a suit?"

"I don't own one that fits," I replied.

He reached in his pocket and said, "Here's a hundred dollars. Go buy yourself a suit, a shirt, a tie, dress shoes and socks. You need to be well dressed in this business. Starting tomorrow, you're going to be a sales and promotion man. Your territory is going to be east to State College, north to Erie, south to Parkersburg, West Virginia, west into Youngstown, Ohio and some parts of the outskirts of the city."

The first day on my new job in a new dark blue suit and black shoes and brand new briefcase, I made my first call on a record store in Pittsburgh's Beechview neighborhood. Driving in Pittsburgh was still stressful. I wasn't at all familiar with the outskirts of the city.

Pittsburgh is made up of many ethnic neighborhoods— Irish, Polish, German and Italian, mostly. My first stop was a small mom-and-pop record shop owned by an Italian family who lived above the store, which was common with small shop owners. They had the most beautiful daughter, who was a few years older than me. George Bodnar, who used to call on this account, told me that she was a knockout who wouldn't give the time of day to any of the salesmen, let alone me. "How old are you kid? 19?" He told me she was stuck up and I shouldn't even try to make out with her. "She is too high class for you," he laughed

I entered the store and introduced myself as the new salesperson from Record Distributors. The mother said to me, "Wait, I will get my daughter. She will place the order." As I looked at all the classical records in the bins, I guessed the parents weren't much into rock music so they let her talk to the salesmen to place their orders. As I nervously waited for the daughter I opened my briefcase on the record counter away from the cash register. Just then she appeared from another room and as she walked behind the counter across from me, I saw she was just as George described her, maybe even more beautiful. She was probably the most sophisticated-looking girl I had ever seen. I don't know if I was nervous because she was so attractive or because she was my first client.

As she approached me, she said, "Are you new at this job? I've never seen you before."

I just stared at her in awe because I never stood so close to anyone who looked like her. I couldn't take my eyes off her. She looked like Sophia Loren. It must have been obvious to her because she walked from the other side of the counter to the side where I was and said, "Just calm down, don't be so nervous."

She was trying to help me. I knew nothing about selling. I had no training and I guess she could sense that I was new. She explained a few tricks of the trade to me and I soon felt settled and a little relieved. After I seemed to calm down, she said, "Just tell me about your new releases and I will let you know if they would sell here. We have a unique clientele who prefers classical music to rock. But we do stock some of the better selling hits. When will the new Buddy Holly LP be released? You should start by taking our inventory of your labels and let me know what we are low on. Then I will place an order."

I walked over to where they displayed their rock music and took an inventory as she suggested and when I finished I handed it to her. I tried hard not to stare at her but it was hard to look away. She was not only gorgeous but also extremely well dressed.

After filling out my order she handed it back to me and said "Here's your order. That wasn't too bad now was it? There is just one other thing I have to say—you dress really well for this job and you look good. But from now on, when you wear a dark blue suit and black shoes, do *not* wear white socks."

She said it in such a helpful way it was like having an older sister help you get ready for your first school dance. I felt kind of stupid, but she had given me my first order. As I left she said, "I will see you when you come back in two weeks and don't forget—no white socks with a suit…ever!"

"Never," I repeated as I waved good bye.

I was always grateful to her for pointing that out to me. Even today, I don't mind people telling me something that would help me improve what I do. Some people get upset and insulted if you try to point out something like that, but it never bothered me.

There was a Murphy's 5 & 10 store a few doors down from her shop. So what did I do? I bought a pair of black socks for forty-nine cents and took the white socks off forever. I was proud of myself for making that first sale and I learned a lot. But the biggest lesson I learned that first day had nothing to do with the record business.

The Penn Boys' First Recording

I couldn't wait to get home from my sales and promotion work to rehearse and practice singing the songs I had written with The Penn Boys. One of the songs was titled "Gonna Have a Party." That was the record Zeke Nicholas heard on WCAE, which prompted him to book us at the Irwin VFW. I arranged the music with guitarist Carl Thompson from Pitcairn and I also sang in the group.

I used the money I saved working for Tim at Record Distributors to record the Penn Boys at Gateway Records, then I sent the master to Queen Pressing in Cincinnati to press one thousand singles at a cost of 21 cents each. I released and distributed the record myself, taking it to the jocks I knew from the local dances. They gave the record quite a lot of airplay and The Penn Boys the recognition I wanted. Every time they played the record, the disc jockey would mention our names on the air. People thought we were making a lot of money. We weren't.

But whenever I did have money I would take the group into another studio to record. We used any place that looked like it could be a studio—basements, clubs or church halls. We even recorded in a barn in the North Hills area of Pittsburgh owned by a symphony orchestra musician who heard we were looking for a place to record and offered us his studio, which was in the barn. We recorded for anyone who had a tape recorder.

I secured airplay for "Gonna Have a Party" in every market I took it to. I was promoting my own product while getting paid to promote Record Distributor records for Tim Tormey. Tim knew this and helped me. I traveled West Virginia, parts of Ohio, upstate New York, and throughout Pennsylvania promoting the records, making friends with every small jock in every small town I worked and they played my records.

I got so busy I had to drop out of The Penn Boys as a performer, but I continued to manage the group.

National Record Mart

My biggest account was the National Record Mart chain. National Record Mart was owned by the Shapiro brothers, Sam and Howard, better known as Howie and Jason. The Shapiro Brothers were feared by their competitors. They owned 34 stores in the Tri State area surrounding Pittsburgh and they were good at what they did. They knew how to handle the record manufacturers because they owned a record company and distributorship in addition to their retail operation. Their main office housed the largest record store I had ever seen.

Their father started the business during the Great Depression. The Shapiro's uncle was a juke box operator and he would give his old records to their father. The sons, Sam, Howie and Jason would sell the used jukebox records at his store. From that fledgling operation, the father and his three sons started National Record Mart with one store.

After serving in World War II, the Shapiro boys returned home to start opening more stores with the help of another area veteran, Edward J DeBartolo. DeBartolo started building shopping centers in city suburbs to accommodate the urban expansion prompted by returning GI's. Looking to expand National Record Marts into the suburbs as well, they struck a deal with DeBartolo to put a record store in all his shopping centers. In this way, they were able to eventually pen 34 stores.

Gateway Recording Studio

The Shapiro's leased the third floor of their Forbes Avenue National Record Mart building to Gateway Records. It was both a recording studio and a record label. The Shapiro's went into partnership with its owner, Bobby Schactner, but it didn't work out. I liked Bobby and I thought he was a good business man. But he was underfinanced and he always had cash flow problems. Still, his studio became *the* place to record for Pittsburgh acts. Anytime I was close to Forbes Avenue National Record Mart, I dropped by Gateway studio to see who was recording. By then I was managing groups other than The Penn Boys and I was using Gateway to record them. I spent every dime I earned recording these groups for my label.

Bobby Schactner was always in need of money, so he would offer me deals. "If you pay me in advance, I'll give you a free hour of studio time. Or if you can guarantee me 3 hours of studio time each week and pay me in advance, I will only charge you for 2 hours."

The Musicians Union in those days set a minimum of three hours as the length of a standard recording session. The union would occasionally pay a surprise visit to the studio to see if I was using union musicians. Since I had hopes that a major label would eventually pick up the recordings, I had to comply with Union rules. Theoretically, radio stations were not to play non-union records. To my knowledge, nobody ever checked, but I didn't want to take any chances, so I went with union guys. Bobby Schactner taught me a few shortcuts to overcome that problem. "Don't worry, I'll fix that," would become a saying that he used.

Bobby Vinton

One day, while I was talking with Johnny Bodnar outside of my office, someone drove up to the curb in a new Plymouth convertible. Out jumped a young, good-looking guy who walked right up to Johnny and me. "Hi my name is Bobby Vinton and

I'm backing up a band for Tim Tormey's concert. Where can I find him?"

"He's not in right now, but he'll be back soon. Why not wait around?" John said.

"Okay. What do you guys do?" He said.

John responded, "I take care of the stock room and Pat here is our promotion and sales guy."

I put my hand out and said, "Hi, I'm Pat DiCesare." Although Bobby had a band and was quite popular in Pittsburgh, I had never heard of him and I was not impressed.

He said, "Did you ever hear of me? I go to Duquesne School of Music and I have a great band. I'm looking to record. Do you know what I could do to get a record out?"

John pointed to me and said, "Talk to him. He has a record out right now that's getting a lot of air play."

"You do! What's the record?"

"I'm Spinning by The Del Vikings."

"I know that song. Is that you? What did you have to do with it?"

"I wrote both sides."

"I have two great songs that I'd love to record. Could you get me on a label?" He asked.

"I don't know anything about you." I pointed out. "What are your songs like? Do you have a demo tape with you?"

"Well, not exactly. You see, I am not a rock act. I have a big band. My father has had a big band for years. I sing and play standards and songs of today and I have two songs to record. I didn't write them, but every time I play these songs with my band I get a great reaction. They've been hits before."

"I don't know if I'm interested in songs that have been released before, what are the titles?

"You've probably heard of the Ray Charles version of "Halleluiah I Love Her So,*"* but I do a different version, an instrumental version."

"Why would anyone want to buy your version when they can get Ray Charles?"

"You're right. It's just a good B side. People like the way I do it. But I also do an old standard called "Twilight Time" that people really like."

"Yeah, I know that song. I've played it many times on the accordion. It's an old standard. I think you might be right. It would be something different for me to record. I'll tell you what. I will go to one of your shows. If I like it, I'll record it on my label, providing you pay for your musicians. I'll pay for the studio time, the mastering and the pressings. I will promote and distribute it…if I like it. Deal?"

"It's a deal." We shook hands and he left. That weekend, I went to a hotel in town where he was playing. He played "Twilight Time" right away. I liked the arrangement and stayed to hear more, including "Halleluiah I Love her So." The audience loved him. He was a great performer who I thought had potential.

At the time, I was forming a new record label and was thinking of names for my new venture. I wanted to sign Bobby to a multi-record deal, so to impress him I called my new label Bobby Records.

Bobby brought Jim Drake and a lot of great musicians from Duquesne School of Music to the session. *Twilight Time* came out great. He played the song in the style of Jimmy Dorsey, whom we represented and I liked. I sent the masters out to Queen Pressing and ordered a thousand 45s.

I felt that no disc jockey would play "Halleluiah I Love Her So," so I pushed "Twilight Time" as our A side. I got some good reaction from the out-of-town jocks. Bob Campo at WOMP in Wheeling told me, "Hey, I think it's a great song. I've seen Bobby perform. He's great and the girls love him. You might have something here." This is exactly what I thought. I figured if I kept pushing the record and got some Pittsburgh jocks to play it, I would have a hit.

Just as the promotion was starting to pay off and we started to get strong regional airplay I got a call from my number one guy, DJ Bob Campo from Wheeling.

"Hey, buddy, I have some bad news for you."

"What's so bad, Bob?"

"I hate to tell you this friend, but The Platters just released, "Twilight Time." It's the B-side of "Out of My Mind.""

I was dismayed. Buck Ram, the Platters' manager, had written and recorded "Twilight Time" in 1946 with his brother and cousin in a group called "The Three Suns." I loved the song and the group because they featured an accordion. This is how I knew the song so well—I used to get requests for the song when I played it on the accordion with my uncle.

Now, here it was twelve years later, Buck had The Platters in the studio recording "Out Of My Mind" for Mercury Records, and he recorded their version of "Twilight Time" as the B-side. It was just filler. The Platters needed another song and Buck Ram mentioned "Twilight Time" and they recorded it on the spot. Mercury released the single and pushed "Out Of My Mind." But, Buck's secretary liked "Twilight Time" better. She talked Dick Clark into playing it on his TV show. The next day the orders came pouring in. It was an overnight hit, a million-seller. No one would play Bobby's version after that. But The Platters record was great. It deserved to be a hit.

"Twilight Time" was heartache and took its toll both financially and mentally for me. But, that's the way this business is. It's a crap shoot.

Payola

By now, "Rock 'n Roll," a phrase coined by Cleveland disc jockey Alan Freed, had become mainstream music. Freed had the power to "make or break" an artist. The record companies offered him bribes or free appearances by their artists if he would play their record. Freed put 10 or 12 acts together on a bus and sent them from city to city to perform at small concert halls. So in this way, he was also the father of modern rock tours as we know them today.

It was widely known to record companies Freed would accept money to play their records, which the government called "payola." It was illegal, but still the companies had to pay for the play. Some jocks, like Alan Freed, demanded part of the songwriter's credit and were actually listed on the record label as a co-writer. It was common for independent record companies to sign new artists under these terms. The artists were so excited to get a record deal they would sign anything without even reading the contract. Another method of payola was to give the jock or the record company a lucrative piece of the publishing.

Giving jocks free records was yet another form of payola. Record company owners would tell the jock, "If you play the record we will give you a thousand free records." The disc jockey could sell them to a record store at a discounted price, usually 50 cents instead of the 60 cents they paid distributors— free vacations, color TV's, even hookers were on the menu for a cooperative DJ.

Each record distributor had a promotion department. The promotion men (and later, women) would go to the program director at each radio station to get their records played and pay the jocks under the table if necessary. Not all the jocks were on the take. There were some honest jocks who wouldn't take money and stations that wouldn't tolerate it. Joe Averbach had his own payola system. He would tell me, "I'm not paying for a promotion man. I just find out which DJ is on the take and I pay him two hundred dollars a week to play my records. I have different jocks at different stations." If those jocks made his record a hit the other jocks at the station and in the area would have to play it, too. It worked for him.

In 1958, the federal government started looking into the payola business and started interviewing the bigger jocks. The two biggest national jocks were Dick Clark and Alan Freed. Dick Clark was clean. The biggest offender was Alan Freed. In 1959, he was convicted of payola and given a suspended jail sentence along with some fines. He died in 1965 from alcohol abuse. He was one of the original inductees into the Rock and Roll Hall of Fame.

Go for Your Dreams

One day at work in 1958, Tim told me that Lou Boorstein, who lived in New York and was the owner of our company, was coming into town for a special meeting and a big announcement. We thought our company was doing well and that perhaps he was going to expand. He did come in, not to expand the business, but to close it.

Tim asked me to drive Lou to the airport after the meeting and even though he just terminated our jobs, I felt privileged to do it. He was a man I had never seen but only heard about and I was in awe of him. He was an important person in the record business—the business in which I wanted to be successful.

During the drive Boorstein asked me "What are you going to do now for a job?"

"I don't know yet." I replied. I had no idea he was going to close the business without any warning. I had a sick feeling. My mother's words came to mind, *Pat, why don't you become a schoolteacher?* I remembered those words all my life and many times I regretted not listening to her. I was 19 now. What was I to do for the rest of my life?

"I am going to give you some sound advice," Lou said. "Don't ever work for anyone. Open your own business. Be in control of your own destiny. Don't be dependent on anyone else. If you want to be successful, do the things that other people won't or don't want to do."

I didn't know if I really understood what he was telling me but I respected and looked up to him as a big deal in the record business. Just the fact that he lived in New York was big enough for me.

As I dropped Mr. Boorstein off at the airport he wished me luck and said, "Don't forget what I told you. Go for your dreams. You're young. You can do it."

Driving back to our office on the North Side I thought perhaps I should have taken the job at Westinghouse Air Brake in Wilmerding that Bob Greene's dad offered me. I would have still been working. *What a failure I am*, I thought. *I quit the Holiday House, I quit college, I quit Westinghouse Electric, and now I've lost this job. I have no money and no place to go.*

I felt the same hurt I felt when my girlfriend Donna's mother asked me to leave their house because I wasn't their kind, and when Miss Bierer asked me to resign as president of the debate team. I'll never amount to anything, I feared.

Decca Records

A few weeks later I got a call from the General Manager at Decca Records on Penn Avenue. Decca was the parent company of Coral and Brunswick that I had worked for with Tim.

He offered me a job at Decca in sales because Tim Tormey had given me a good recommendation. I took the job as their sales person in the outlying territory surrounding Pittsburgh.

I liked working for Decca. It was a large company, more organized than the independent labels. They had a large catalogue of great LP's. I did particularly well selling their Christmas music. Bing Crosby's "White Christmas" probably sold more records than any other song in the history of the recording business.

Decca was a conservative company with numerous country western artists like Patsy Cline and Webb Pierce, as well as older adult-oriented artists like Bing Crosby and Sammy Davis Jr. But even though I liked Decca and was treated royally, I preferred working for the independent labels because they had more rock and roll acts. Decca did have Ricky Nelson, but I never considered Ricky a true rock act.

After six months at Decca I got a call from Tim Tormey, who had moved back to New York. "Pat," he said, "I'm opening a distributorship in New York for Bobby Klien and Brud Osseroff. They're expanding their Mobile Records business and opening an office here in New York. I've agreed to run it and I want you to work for me. Would you be willing to move to New York? I think you'll like it here."

"That's good enough for me," I replied. I packed my car and drove to New York. It was the summer of 1959.

New York, 1959

For nearly a year I lived in a hotel on West 72 and Broadway and never met the people who lived to the left or right of me. In a city of twelve million people I never made a friend. Everyone seemed to be in a hurry in New York. I was just a small town guy in one of the biggest cities in the world and I couldn't wait to get back to Pittsburgh.

I didn't like New York. I told Tim I was thinking about quitting and moving back to Pittsburgh. He understood and asked me to stay with it for just a while longer because he was working on something that would be good for the two of us. I stayed. A few months later, Tim announced that he was moving back to Pittsburgh to open up another record distributorship for Lou Boorstien called Cosnat Records and he could me get me more money than I was making in New York. So back to Pittsburgh we went.

I was glad to get back home.

Cosnat Distributing, Pittsburgh, 1960

At Cosnat, my job was the same as it had been for every other distributor I had worked for—sales and promotion. It required me drive to places like Youngstown, Erie, Johnstown, State College, Wheeling, Clarksburg, Parkersburg, Fairmont, and every little two-bit town in between. I also got the downtown Pittsburgh accounts, which I shared with Tim, including National Record Marts. This made me a pretty big deal in the Pittsburgh record business.

I didn't mind the traveling, but my favorite accounts were in downtown Pittsburgh because that's where the action was. My biggest clients were the Shapiro's at National Record Mart.

I always looked forward to calling on Kaufmann's Department Store. It was the most prestigious of all accounts. Its record department was managed by an older, unmarried Jewish woman by the name of Ida Ginsburg. She had a reputation for being difficult to deal with and tough on salesmen. All the other sales and promotion men feared her. I didn't. She liked Tim so that made me okay. She called me "Tim's boy."

On the other hand, I did not like going to Gimbel's downtown, the second largest of Pittsburgh's three big department stores (Horne's was third). Gimbel's had a record buyer named Marion, a sophisticated, attractive, and well-dressed middle-aged blonde. One day Marion called Tim and asked him to replace me as his sales rep for Gimbel's. She would rather have someone else call on her. Tim asked why. At that time, I had an allergy problem. I still do. I had to take allergy shots to desensitize myself. My allergies caused my nasal membranes to swell, which caused my voice to sound nasally. I always sounded as though I had a cold. That bothered Marion and she didn't like being around me because of that.

Tim didn't want to confront me with such a sensitive issue. He knew I felt self-conscious about it. So he just let me keep the account. When Marion told me about it I was crushed. I went to Tim and asked to be replaced by George Bodnar. I felt relieved to be rid of her even though she had cost me a prestigious account and a big commission. It dampened my enthusiasm and I crawled back into my shell again. I became reluctant to meet or talk to anyone.

Because of that, Tim graciously let me be the rep for his biggest account - National Record Mart, and share in the commissions. That helped to lift my spirits.

Chapter Seven
A Desperate Gamble Pays Off

Sly and the Family Stone: Nov 28, 1970

In the summer of 1970 I started putting together a special Thanksgiving concert I called the Shower of Stars. I've always regarded Thanksgiving weekend from Wednesday through Sunday to be the best days in show business. College kids go home for the weekend on Wednesday and by Friday night they're bored to death. They're ready to get out of the house and have fun. And what's more fun than a rock concert? I always had a Thanksgiving concert at the Civic Arena that weekend and it was always a sellout. If I couldn't get a major artist to play the date I would put together several smaller name acts and call it a Shower of Stars concert.

Wally Amos, a tall, dapper African-American gentleman, was the agent for the William Morris Agency in New York, the biggest talent agency in America. I first met Wally in Pittsburgh when he attended one of Tim's concerts at the Syria Mosque. Wally handled William Morris's top artists and everyone respected him. He was known for baking chocolate chip cookies and passing them around the William Morris office. Everybody loved Wally Amos's cookies. Eventually, he turned that hobby into a successful worldwide business—Famous Amos.

Wally's assistant at William Morris was a Hispanic young man named Hector Morales, who was responsible for screening Wally's calls. Hector started out working in the mailroom—a classic way to advance your career in entertainment agencies.

Music mogul and billionaire David Geffen started in the William Morris mail room and so did Hector.

Trying to reach Wally by phone was a daily chore for me. I would call him five times a day—unsuccessfully. He never returned my calls. I needed to get the availabilities of his artists for my Thanksgiving Shower of Stars show at the Civic Arena so I had to be persistent. After numerous frustrating conversations with the William Morris receptionist she finally put me through to Wally's office.

It was Hector Morales who answered. Hector was friendly and patient, the opposite of Wally, who seemed constantly irritated and impatient. I didn't particularly like talking to Wally, but I had to. He controlled too many top acts that I needed.

I explained the situation to Hector. "Hector," I said, "If you can get me to Wally, I will do you many favors. Whenever you have a new act you need a date for within a hundred miles of Pittsburgh I will get your act booked. When you need to fill a college date in the fall, I will help you. Okay? I book a lot of colleges and promote a lot of shows and I can help you. All I ask is that you answer my calls and give me your available dates, or put me on the line with Wally."

I understood agents' problems. I was an agent myself, as well as a promoter. Agents were always in need of fill-in dates that made routing sense for their acts on the road. If an act was going from Buffalo to Cleveland, for example, I could find them a fill-in date somewhere in between, even if I had to promote it myself in some two-bit town.

"Okay, Pat, thanks. I will pass that on to Wally and let him know you called."

Days went by without a callback. I needed those acts. So I called Hector again and he took the call.

"Hector, *please* tell Wally that I am planning a Shower of Stars Show at the Civic Arena in Pittsburgh the week of Thanksgiving. I need to know of any availabilities he may have that weekend. The show is only four months away and I have to lock in some acts now. I'm starting to get nervous."

"Okay, Pat. I hear you. I will tell Wally, You still have a lot of time."

But I didn't have a lot of time. I was getting dangerously close to the date and I still didn't have my acts.

Hector advised me, "You need to come to New York, Pat. Get to know all the agents here at the agency and the other agencies in town. That will let them put a face with the voice and they'll be more willing to do business with you."

"Okay, Hector, I'll take your advice. I'll come to New York and I'll have a gift for you when I get there."

"Really? What have you got?"

"I'm not telling you. It's a surprise."

It was a surprise to me, too, because I hadn't even thought of it until that moment. I was about to take a desperate gamble.

I had recently taken a call at my office from a girl in Chicago who said she wanted to meet me. I quickly determined that she was a groupie who wanted to meet me because I was a promoter.

"If I come to Pittsburgh, will you spend some time with me?" she asked, making it clear that she was willing to do anything I wanted. "Could I spend the weekend with you when you have some concerts scheduled? I want to meet some of the bands. I'll make it worth your while."

I was married by then and I certainly was not interested in anything like that for myself. But Hector was single and while I was speaking with him on the phone an idea popped into my head. I called the girl back. "How would you like to meet a big-time New York agent who knows *all* the top bands?"

"Who? What's his name? Which bands?"

"Take my word for it. He's a big deal and I'm going to help you out. Instead of flying to Pittsburgh, fly to New York. I'm going to New York to see this guy myself and I'll introduce you. I'll be flying home the next day, but you can stay longer. He'll show you around New York and take you to meet his acts."

"That sounds great, okay, when?"

"I'll get back to you and let you know."

Then I called Hector. "When will you have a couple of free days and nights to entertain a special visitor?"

"I can't promise you when I'll have time off," Hector replied, "but you can come up to meet the agents. I'll take you with me to a few showcases and we can get together for dinner." That was good enough for me.

I called the girl back. "Book your plane and hotel. Plan to spend two or three nights in the City. I will call you at your hotel and arrange for you to meet Hector. You'll like him. He's a nice guy and he'll introduce you to all the bands you want to meet."

I had never arranged for an agent to meet a girl before and I was taking a huge chance. I didn't know this girl. I didn't even know what she looked like. It was crazy, but I was desperate.

"What do you look like?" I asked her.

"Let's just say that your friend is going to be very happy when he sees me," she assured me.

"I'm taking a big risk here," I told her.

"Don't worry. You're doing the right thing."

So I flew to New York that week from Pittsburgh and she flew in from Chicago, I got in on Thursday and she was booked to arrive on Friday. Unfortunately, I had to fly back to Pittsburgh on Friday, so she would be arriving after my departure. Still, by then Hector (I hoped) would be so curious about my gift that he would be eager to take her call.

When I got to the William Morris office in Manhattan I told him, "I don't have your gift with me. But you'll be getting a call after I leave New York tomorrow. *Make sure* you answer your private line and be available for the weekend."

As I hoped, Hector's curiosity was up. "Come on Pat, you have to tell me what to expect. Is it a girl? Is that it? You got me a hooker?"

"No, she is not a hooker. But you will like her." That's all I would tell him. That's all I *could* tell him!

I spent the rest of the day meeting with agents in the city. After dinner that night with Hector we made the rounds of a few clubs to see some of his bands. I never really liked that part of the business. No agent likes to go to clubs to listen to new bands.

The next day, as I was leaving for the airport, I told Hector, "I hope you enjoy your gift."

First thing Monday morning, Hector called. He sounded ecstatic, "Pat, Pat, where did you find her? I think I'm in love. She's beautiful. We did things that I didn't even know two people could do."

"So you liked her?"

"Yeah, she's great. I'm flying her back to New York again. Now…I've got some good news for *you*. I am now your agent. You don't have to speak with Wally anymore. Let's talk about your Thanksgiving show. I might have something for you."

My gamble with the girl had paid off.

"We have Sly and the Family Stone at Madison Square Garden on Friday November 27, the day after Thanksgiving. I have several other offers for Saturday November 28, but it's open as of now. If you want I can steer Sly to Pittsburgh that night.'

I was elated. Sly was the hottest act I could have booked. The Woodstock film had come out and Sly's performance made him the hottest act in the country. "Sly would be fantastic!" I said. "He'll sell the place out on his own. I don't even need another act. When can you let me know?"

"Before you get too excited I need to tell you we've been having a little trouble with Sly not showing up on some dates. I wouldn't worry, because his whole family travels with him and they'll make sure he shows up. I'll send you the contract. Sign it and get it right back to me quickly. I want to get it to Sly for his signature, too."

I wanted to get the ball rolling to keep Sly from backing out of the date. I knew Hector could book the date in other cities and I did not want to lose this show. Hector called me later that day to confirm the date and tell me I could start advertising and selling tickets. So I put the show on sale and it sold well immediately.

Then I got a call from a reporter at the *Pittsburgh Post-Gazette*. "Pat," he said, "Do you think Sly will show up for your concert at the arena?"

"Why certainly. Why wouldn't he? Why do you ask?" I had never been asked such a question before.

"Because several cities have reported he didn't show or he went on late, and on some dates he left before the show was even over."

"Well, I am not worried. He will perform." I was glad the show was selling well, but if reporters started writing stories it could hurt.

The next day I got a call from Charlie Strong, the arena manager, "Pat, what's the word on Sly and the Family Stone? I hear rumors that he isn't showing up at his concerts."

"I've heard that, too. He is playing Madison Square Garden the night before our show. William Morris wouldn't book him if they didn't think he would show."

"All the same, I am concerned. I've had a call from the mayor's office. They heard about Sly's no-shows, too, and they want to know what we intend to do about it if he's a no-show at the Arena. How will you refund money? Will you refund parking fees? What if it prompts a riot in the Arena? City Hall thinks this could be a dangerous situation and that we'll need police dogs and more uniformed police officers. I need answers."

Off the top of my head I came up with the answer he needed. "I'll go to New York for the Madison Square Garden show the night before our concert. I'll stay at Sly's hotel and fly back to Pittsburgh on Sly's plane the next day. I will personally make sure that Sly and the Family Stone shows up in Pittsburgh and plays the show." That seemed to satisfy Charlie.

Again I called Hector. "Hector, I need two tickets to the Sly and the Family Stone show at The Garden for you and me. I want you to take me back stage after the show to meet his road manager. Book me at his hotel and hook me up with his family. I'll get on the plane with them to Pittsburgh the next day. I am going to stick to Sly Stone like glue until he does our show."

Hector agreed. He got the tickets and booked the hotel.

In the meantime, I continued to put together the show and manage the promotion and all the details that go into putting on a great show at the Pittsburgh Civic Arena headlined by one the hottest acts in America. Confident that all the necessary arrangements had been made, I was able to leave for New York the day before the show in order to safely escort its star back to Pittsburgh with me and put him and his band on that stage, intact and on time.

After taking a cab from the airport, checking into the hotel in Manhattan, and having dinner alone, Hector met me at the hotel and we walked the few blocks to Madison Square Garden.

"I've arranged for you to meet Sly's road manager after the show." He informed me, "And I've got tickets for us right up front to watch the concert. "

If there was anything I hated it was sitting in the audience watching a concert. I never did that at any of my shows. This was business, not pleasure. To me a concert was work, not entertainment. Nevertheless, there I was, reluctantly sitting in the audience at Madison Square Garden with the agent who had made my Thanksgiving weekend show possible, waiting to see the star who was to headline it.

At 8:15—15 minutes late—the house lights dimmed, the audience started screaming, and the announcer shouted, "Ladies and gentlemen, Sly and the Family Stone!" The band, minus Sly, took the stage. They looked like stars, but the real star of the show was nowhere to be seen. After The Family Stone had played for 30 minutes without him I was worried! Finally—and to my relief— Sly sauntered out onto the stage to perform a full show to a wildly enthusiastic audience, and for the first time since that reporter's disturbing phone call I felt certain my show would go off as planned.

Backstage after the show, Hector introduced me to Sly's father as the promoter of the Pittsburgh show the next evening. As delicately as possible I told him I was there to escort Sly to Pittsburgh the next day to make sure he showed up.

"What are you talking about? He was here tonight, wasn't he? Didn't you watch the show?" Obviously, the man had an attitude. I didn't care to meet Sly but his road manager insisted. Sly appeared to be a little spaced out but he said nothing to me to indicate I would have a problem with him.

I arranged with the road manager to meet him and the band in the hotel lobby at 9:30 in the morning to check out and take two limos to the airport for the 12:00 flight to Pittsburgh. I was in the lobby waiting for them by 9:30 but by 10:30 no one had yet shown up. By then we had only 90 minutes left to get to the airport and get on the plane. Again, I was worried.

The father was the first to appear and he still had an attitude. The band showed up a few minutes later and I dispatched them in the first limo off the airport.

Finally, at eleven o'clock, Sly himself strolled through the lobby with his arms swinging wildly, wearing a fur coat and a furry hat over multi-colored stripped bell bottoms. He was quite a spectacle. His father asked him, "Are you ready to go?"

He nodded at me he said, "Yeah, man. Let's do it!" I thought my problems were over.

We arrived at the airport just a few minutes before takeoff, checked in at the gate, and started to board the plane, with Sly in front of me and his father behind me. Then halfway up the steps, Sly stopped and turned around and looked at me. "You go on," he said. "I'll be right back. I've gotta do something."

I was startled. "What are you talking about? Where are you going? The plane is about to leave." Without another word he pushed back past me down the steps. I couldn't believe it. I was watching Sly walk away. "Don't follow him," his father ordered me. "If you follow him you'll ruin everything and he won't go to Pittsburgh for sure. Go ahead and get on the plane."

Seeing all this happening, the stewardess at the top of the steps said, "You all have to get on board now if you are coming with us." Sly had disappeared, his father was yelling at me to get on the plane, the stewardess was about to close the door, what was I to do?

"If we get on this plane without Sly, how will he get to Pittsburgh?" I asked his father,

"He'll take another plane."

"But his ticket is for this flight."

"There's nothing I can do. Sly does what he wants to do."

I had no choice. We boarded the plane...without Sly. After all my precautions and efforts it looked like Sly and the Family Stone would be no-shows for my show after all. How would he get there now? Could he even get another flight to Pittsburgh in time? I was worried sick, but there was nothing I could do until we arrived in Pittsburgh, and his father was no help.

I called Hector from a pay phone the minute I was off the plane and told him what had happened. "I don't know what to tell you, Pat," he said. "Let me make some calls."

I decided to have the band do a sound check in the afternoon without Sly. That was not unusual. Many headliners did not go to a sound check. They left that up to others in the group.

I had an office at the arena behind the stage and I hid out there from the time I got in from the airport until the afternoon sound check. At that point I had told no one that Sly was not in Pittsburgh. The band completed their sound check at 5:00. Three hours until show time and I still had no idea if and how Sly would show up. Again I called Hector. "Did you hear from Sly?"

"Not yet. This isn't good for any of us. When the word spreads about this no one will want to book him anymore."

"Tell me about it. I wish I hadn't either."

Time was going by fast and still there was no word from Sly. Another call to Hector. "What am I supposed to do? It's almost time for the arena to open the doors and let people in. They're lined up all around the building and the arena management wants me to open early. It's cold out there. I had to assure Charlie Strong that Sly was here. Now I've got to tell him the truth."

"Don't do that yet," Hector said.

"I have to. His staff is outside my office, they keep knocking on the door. They know something is wrong. Where the hell is he?"

I heard another knock. "Pat, this is Whitey. We're going to open the doors and let the people in. Is that okay with you and the act?" he yelled through the closed door. I thought for a moment. If I have to cancel the show, I should do it now, before they open the doors. I had never canceled a show in my life. Whitey knocked again. "Pat, can I open the doors? Is something wrong?"

"No, Whitey, go ahead and open the doors."

With thousands of eager concert-goers pouring through the doors the star they were there to see was still missing in action.

At 7:45 the band's limos pulled up to the backstage door. I got a call from Sgt. Bill Evans. "The act just pulled in, I'm going to let them drive through. I was starting to worry they weren't coming. I'm sure glad they're here."

A sense of relief washed over me. I rushed out of my office to meet the limos. The band climbed out but there was still no Sly. I approached his father. "Where is Sly? What are we going to do?"

"We'll put the band on like we did at Madison Square Garden and have them play the band tracks to all the hits until he gets here."

"And what do we do if he doesn't get here?" Without replying, he just turned and walked away. I realized that no one had any power over Sly, not even his father.

I walked back to my office and asked Joe Brown to find Sgt. Jim Patterson of the City Police and bring him to my office. I told my brother, Mike, to start the show as late as possible and to tell Chuck Brinkman, KQV's top jock, to let the DJ's talk as much as they wanted. I hated having the station jocks emcee a show because some of them talked too much. But I needed to kill time. I still had no idea if and when Sly was coming. I knew I was in trouble and if he didn't show I would have to refund all the money to the ticket holders and pay all the workers anyway--police, stage hands, teamsters, ushers, ticket-takers, limo drivers, caterers, everybody. It would be a huge loss.

I would even have to pay Sly and the Family Stone! There was no guarantee in the contract they would actually perform and they could always claim that Sly was sick and was unable to perform, which would be considered an Act of God and for which I could not sue for damages, Besides, I could never sue a William Morris act because I would never get another one. There was no getting around it. It looked like I was screwed.

I called Sgt. Jim Patterson to my office. "Jim I have a problem, Sly isn't here yet. He's supposed to be on a flight from New York and should be at the airport soon. I need you to arrange for a police escort to the arena and get him here as fast as you can. Can you do that?"

"I knew something was wrong," he replied. "I just felt it. Let's see what we can do. The airport is controlled by Allegheny County and that's the Sheriff's jurisdiction. I know some of those guys. Let me give them a call."

He left and called me a few minutes later. "Okay Pat, you've got your police escort. What flight is he on?"

"I don't know. To tell you the truth, I don't know if he's on any flight at all. But that has to be our secret. Let's see if he gets off the next plane from New York and if the deputies can get him here on time."

"That's a tough order, but if he shows up, we'll get him here."

The DJs stalled as long as possible. I went to Sly's father. "Is the band ready to go on?"

"Yeah, let's do it." I walked up the stairs at the back of the stage and motioned to Chuck Brinkman to announce the act.

The spotlights were blinding me and I couldn't see the audience but I could hear Chuck say, "And now the moment we've all been waiting for—Sly and the Family Stone." The crowd went wild as the band took the stage, just as they did in New York. For 45 minutes they played the instrumental tracks to their songs without any emotion. Maybe they were as concerned as I was and wondered what was going on with their brother. They were probably fed up with him, too.

The crowd was getting impatient. If I had known this would happen I would have put a few opening acts on this show. Why didn't the Family learn some different songs…or at least sing, I thought as I walked off the stage and back towards my office. Charlie Strong came walking up to me, "Pat, why doesn't Sly go on?"

This is it, I thought, *I'll have to stop the show*. The stress was killing me. It was the worst moment of my career.

And at that very moment I spotted Jim Patterson running toward me from the wings. "Pat, he's here, he's here. The Deputies have him and they are approaching Gate 5 now. They say he's really out of it."

I couldn't believe it. It was like a western movie when the Calvary shows up at the last minute and rescues the wagon train from being massacred by the Indians. I looked at Gate 5 as the huge door lifted and driving in was the County Police car. Sly wobbled out of the car to the steps leading up to the stage with Jim by his side. Jim leaned in to my ear and said "Pat, this guy is in no condition to perform. It's a miracle he got here at all."

I grabbed Sly by the arm and led him to the stairs at the back of the stage. He staggered and started crawling on his hands and knees up the stage steps. He was obviously high on something. I helped him to his feet and up the steps. When he saw the spotlights on the stage he stopped and looked at me. He could hardly mumble but he managed to say, "Hey, man, where the fuck am I?" He didn't even know what city he was in!

"Pittsburgh!" I shouted, "You're in Pittsburgh!" As he walked onstage and up to the microphone I thought, *he's never going to pull this one off.* He could barely walk.

Somehow he made it to the front of the stage, wobbling left and right like he was about to fall, grabbed the microphone and shouted in a deep booming voice, "Hello, Pittsburgh!" There was a thunderous reaction from the crowd at the sight of their hero in his outlandish clothes there on the stage alive and not-quite-well. But he made it and he saved my show.

I stayed on the side of the stage to watch him perform and I never saw anything like it! He was more powerful than the night before in New York. He and his band put out more energy than I had ever witnessed in my life with any act, bar none. He completely won over that audience. Just when I thought the show was over, he went back for encore after encore. It was amazing.

As relieved as I had ever felt before, I walked back to my office to finish up my paper work, pack my briefcase, and go home to my wife, Kathy. By the time I left through Gate 2 to get in my car the crowd and the band were gone. I saw the cleanup crew sweeping all the debris left behind by 16,000 satisfied customers, thinking, *thank God, it's over.*

The preparations for this show had started so long ago. I wondered where Sly and the Family Stone were playing tomorrow, who is the promoter, was he somewhere in the audience tonight like I had been in the night before, hoping to put Sly on a plane tomorrow and get the man to his show in one piece and on time? All I knew and all I really cared about was that *this* show was over and it worked.

I was back on top of the world again. I now had all the money I needed to pay my Electric Theatre and Rock Falls Park debt, I had a big bank account again, and things were looking up.

I had Rare Earth as the headliner for my Christmas Shower of Stars and ticket sales were going strong. I promised myself I would never again expose myself to such an enormous potential loss for the sake of a drug-addled rock star I couldn't count on. But then again, I am a risk taker. That's what I do. I thought about what Lenny Littman told me when I met him at his cocktail lounge with Tim when I was just starting out in this career at the age of 18, *don't work for anybody but yourself.* Lou Boorstein had given me the same advice.

I keep reminding myself that I am not a school teacher. I am not one of those guys I worked with at Westinghouse. They wanted the sure paycheck. They were happy with that. Although I respected them because that's where most of my family worked, they were slowly strangling themselves to death. I did that, too…for a while. But that was not what I wanted for my life.

So I'm a gambler. I always have been. Promoting concerts was my game, but at heart I was just a gambler, a risk taker, win or lose. And you know what? I wouldn't have it any other way.

Grand Funk Railroad, November 1, 1971

Grand Funk Railroad was booked into the Civic Arena in Pittsburgh for November 1, 1971. I had booked them the previous year to a half-sold out arena, but the Michigan band had since surged in popularity on the strength of several hit singles.

Of course, they had a rider. We were to provide the band and their roadies with a sit-down lunch and dinner.

This was the first time for such an event. Grand Funk was a big act and I wanted to treat them right. However, I had never provided a sit-down dinner backstage for any act and I had no idea what to serve. I had a million other things to think about. The very idea that a promoter was supposed to feed the act a full dinner backstage like it was a restaurant was bullshit. At least, that's what *I* thought.

To make it even more complicated, the members of Grand Funk Railroad were vegetarians. Back then, I didn't know anyone who was a vegetarian or knew anything about vegetarian food. To its credit, the band did provide us with a suggested menu which I gave to my brother Mike with the instructions to, "Find someone who can cook some vegetables." With all the responsibilities I had to fulfill in order to stage a successful show, providing special food for demanding rock stars was one of the most annoying.

So how was I to provide these particular rock stars, who I knew were going to sell out the Arena, with the sit-down lunch and dinner they insisted on? I didn't want to disappoint them. Where was I to find a vegetarian cook in Pittsburgh, Pennsylvania in 1971?

At least Grand Funk's agent was polite about it. He told me the band members weren't too particular, they just wanted some good down-home cooked vegetarian food. One of the requested dishes was eggplant parmesan. Mike knew that Dad could cook eggplant parmesan because it was Mike's favorite dish and Dad had cooked it for him before. But that fact didn't occur to me at all.

On the day of the show, Mike set up a catering area backstage for the act. I was in my usual place—the box office. I seldom went backstage; I never cared to meet the act. I didn't want my picture taken with them and I didn't want autographs. I knew guys who would promote shows for practically nothing just to have their picture taken with the act. I just wanted to get the show on and over. Between the police, the act, the promoter, and Charlie Strong the arena manager, there was too much stress backstage during a show.

I instructed Mike, "Do what you must do to give Grand Funk the vegetarian dinner they want. That's the most important part of the whole show."

This always brought to mind, Tim Tormey's saying, "You are judged as a promoter by what the acts think of the food you provided backstage." If the food is good, you were regarded as a thoughtful promoter who cares more about the act than making money. So in a way, my reputation as a promoter rested in the hands of my brother Mike. I trusted him to secure a professional catering company that knew how to cook vegetarian dishes to do this job. I didn't care about the cost because the show was selling well and would probably be a sellout.

Shortly before the show was to begin, while I was taking care of business with the box office manager, John Woods, his phone rang. It was Richard Irace, the backstage security guy, calling to tell me that the band wanted to see me—now.

"Uh Oh, "I said. "This can't be good." Anytime an act wants to see you before the show it's usually trouble. My first thought was, *I hope Mike didn't screw up the food.* I raced from Gate 2 to Gate 5 backstage, half-way around the arena, wishing it was tomorrow and this show was already over. Ah, but tomorrow would be another show and a whole new set of worries and problems. That's the promotion business.

When I arrived at Gate 5 I spotted Richard. "What's the problem now?" I asked.

"I don't know. The road manager asked me to locate you. He and the band are in the catering area eating," he said.

Oh, Lord, I thought, *they don't like the food. Mike screwed up the catering.* I kicked myself for leaving the most important job of the whole show up to Mike. What did he know about vegetarian food? I hesitated before grabbing the door handle and prepared for the worst.

Reluctantly opening the door, I saw the members of the band eating at the table Mike had set up and out of the corner of my eye, I saw Mike. I pulled him aside anxiously. "What's wrong Mike? Did you screw this up? Who did you get as the caterer?"

"Dad!" he said with a big grin on his face.

"Dad? What do you mean, Dad?"

"Dad's the caterer," Mike said.

"Dad!" I hollered out under my breath, "What the hell does he know about cooking vegetarian? He's the ultimate carnivore.

Why did you give such an important job to Dad? He's not a caterer."

"I didn't know any caterers. Take it easy, everything's fine." Just then, the leader of the band, Mark Farner, walked up to Mike and put his arm around him like *they* were brothers.

"So, this is your brother?" he asked, nodding at me. "This is the promoter?"

"Yes, this is Pat DiCesare, my brother."

Mark gave me a big smile and put his hand out. "Mr. DiCesare," he said, "This is the best eggplant parmesan we've ever had. Who made it?"

"My dad," Mike interjected with an unmistakable air of pride.

"Is he here? I'd like to thank him and tell him what a great job he did. Do you think he could make some more for us to take when we leave? We've never had food this good on the road before."

What a relief! Mike and Mark had become best buddies and the act was happy.

"Why don't you ask him?" Mike answered. "He's the guy over there with the white apron. That's my dad."

Mark walked over to Dad and said, "Sir, I want to shake your hand. That was the best eggplant parmesan I've ever eaten."

Dad grinned and said "Thank-a-you, young-a-man."

If Tim Tormey was correct—that promoters are judged by the quality of their backstage food—I suppose that as far as Grand Funk Railroad was concerned, I had passed the test... thanks to Dad.

Chapter Eight
My First Concert

Youngstown, Ohio

One Saturday night at the end of August 1960, my group of friends in Trafford—Sonny, Cue Ball, Paul Mediate, John Mikan and myself—were hanging out at the V&M Lounge. We were about to call it a night when Sonny announced, "Well, I won't be seeing you guys for a week."

"Why? Where are you going?" I asked.

"College. I start my second year at Youngstown State University this Monday." Youngstown is about 60 miles northwest of Pittsburgh, in Ohio "Pat, why don't you come with me?" he added.

"What are you talking about?"

"Why don't you go back to college? Come with me and start school on Monday."

"I can't do that. Don't you have to register and be accepted? I can't just walk into a college and start classes without applying first." I had already made that mistake back in my Holiday House days when I tried to get into Penn State without going through the admissions process.

"Yes, you can. I know the people at the registration office. You had good grades in high school and you went to Edinboro one summer. They'll take you at YSU, I promise. You talked about becoming an attorney. Here's your chance."

"I don't have any money. I have $80 left over from payday yesterday. That's all I have to my name."

"Don't worry about that. You always wanted to go back to college this is your chance. Come with me on Monday."

He persuaded me. The next day I called Tim Tormey. "Tim I'd like to go back to college at Youngstown. I've always thought about becoming an attorney and the school year is just starting. If you really feel you need me to stay here and work, I'll stay. But I'd like to give it a shot."

He understood. "Since you are going to be living in Youngstown Ohio, why don't you work there for me three days a week? You could still sell and promote records in West Virginia, Ohio and upstate New York and go to classes two days a week. I will pay you $125 a week. You'll need the money," He said.

"That's great, I can do that."

This was turning into a fine opportunity. I had no idea how I would have made the money I needed to pay for school otherwise. So that Monday I drove my 1957 Cadillac Coupe De Ville to Youngstown and met Sonny at the registrar's office. He approached the young lady working behind the counter and introduced me. "This is my friend Pat DiCesare and he wants to go to school here."

"When?" She asked in an irritated voice without even looking up at us.

"Now."

"Is he registered?"

"No, that's what he wants to do now."

"That's not the way it is done around here." She looked up with an incredulous look on her face, as if we were morons. "You need to register in advance and take a test. We have to see a high school transcript. You can't just waltz in here on the first day and expect to walk into a classroom the same day as a student. What's wrong with you? Do you see all those people over there in that line? They're all registered in advance. Who do you think you are anyway? "

I felt like a jerk as I glared at Sonny, ready to let him have a big piece of my mind. It was Penn State all over again, and I knew better. *Why had I let Sonny talk me into this?*

But then the girl behind the counter had a sudden change of heart. She said, "Alright, walk over to Dr. Cheuey's office right now and wait. I'll see what I can do."

We did as she asked. We hadn't waited long when we were called into Dr. Cheuey's office. She listened to Sonny plead my case. He told her I was a good student in high school and would be a model student. She looked at me and said "Okay, we'll take a chance on you based on Sonny's recommendation." She said I would need to have a transcript of my high school grades sent to her office immediately. If my grades were high as I claimed I could stay, but if they weren't, I'd have to leave.

I was able to schedule all my classes on Tuesdays and Thursdays, although I was a little worried that cramming 16 hours of classes into only two classroom days might be too much. But because I was so late registering I was limited to classes that were still available, which meant that my first class started at eight o'clock in the morning and my last class ended at 10 o'clock at night.

On Monday, Wednesday and Friday I would work for Tim. That would leave me Saturday and Sunday to study. My goal was to graduate in three years instead of the usual four, in order to catch up and graduate with Sonny.

Tuesday, May 8, 1962

At the beginning of my second year at YSU I made an appointment to see Dr. Chuey, who was my faculty advisor. I had an idea for her. She asked how she could help me.

"Each semester, we students are charged a $35 activity fee," I began, "and all we get for it are tickets to the football and basketball games. Most of the students don't even attend those events. I was thinking, why can't the school sponsor some music concerts and give the students a choice—tickets to the games or to the concerts?"

Dr. Chuey was intrigued. "That's a very interesting idea, Pat. I've never thought of that. But I have no idea how it could be done. Do you?"

"Yes. I have produced concerts," I replied. I went on to explain how you put a show together.

"That sounds great," she said. "Why don't you put a concert together and the school will sponsor it, as long as you assume all the expenses. It will be your show. If it makes money it's yours, if it loses money, it's your loss. And you must submit the name of the artist you want to promote to me for approval before you sign any contracts."

I suggested The Four Freshman and she approved. I called Capitol Records at Hollywood and Vine and they directed me to their agency in New York. The cost to get the act would be $1500. Other expenses would include the cost of the hall and because YSU did not have an auditorium of sufficient size I would have to rent The Stambaugh Auditorium. Other expenses included, printing tickets, selling tickets, advertising on radio and the newspapers and staffing at the auditorium. My total estimated expenses would be about $4,500.

The manager of Stambaugh Auditorium asked me when I approached him about renting his facility, "Is this show reserved seats or GA? Who is the presenter?"

I didn't know. He could tell I was green so he explained, "With an act like The Four Freshman you should sell only reserved seats. And make yourself the presenter. What is your name?"

"Pat DiCesare."

"Okay, Pat. At this facility, every show must have a presenter. When you do your advertising we want you to use your own name, like *Pat DiCesare Presents The Four Freshmen.*" I liked that. It sounded great. While working for Tim Tormey, it had always been Tim's show. I was only his assistant. But this was *my* show, with my name on it, and that appealed to me.

One of my many responsibilities as the presenter was to set up off-premise ticket sale outlets. I already knew the owners of most of the record stores in the Youngstown area, the biggest being the Record Rendezvous downtown, so I designated that store as my primary outlet. The owners of The Record Rendezvous, however, were small minded—they couldn't understand that I was advertising their name along with my show and bringing traffic into their store. Their attitude was in contrast to National Record Mart in Pittsburgh who actually set up a box office in the back of their main store to attract ticket buyers. As I couldn't afford to pay someone else to sell tickets at the Record Rendezvous I spent every spare moment of my time at the store myself, standing behind a counter, waiting patiently for the occasional ticker-buyer to come in.

During one of those vigils, Bobby Vinton walked into the store. Spotting me, he said, "Pat what are you doing here?" I explained that I was attending the college in town and promoting a The Four Freshman concert.

"Going back to college, huh? But why? That's not going to do you any good. You had it made in the record business. I quit Duquesne, you know. Who needs it?"

Bobby could be difficult to deal with, but he was smart and he was an opportunist. He had taken our Bobby Records recording of "Twilight Time" and shopped it around to other record labels, eventually landing a deal at Epic Records. Bobby was a born promoter. He didn't sit back and leave all the promotion to the record company. He hit the road and did his own promotion.

Now here he was in Youngstown at the Record Rendezvous.

"I've got a new record I'm promoting, Pat, and I need your help. Could you take it around to the radio stations you're connected with and get me some airplay?"

"Bobby I'd love to help you but, I'm losing my shirt here with the Four Freshmen. Maybe when it's over I can help you."

"When would that be?"

"May 8."

"That will be too late."

"What's the title of your song?"

"'Roses are Red.' This is the one, Pat. This is a hit." He gave me a DJ copy of the record and went on his way and the rest—as they say—is history. "Roses are Red" became a smash hit, a standard that is still played and loved by my generation to this day. I didn't talk to Bobby again until years later when we tried to book him at The Stanley Theatre in Pittsburgh and he wouldn't give me a date. He was still mad at me because I wouldn't help him promote "Roses Are Red." I guess he'd forgotten that I gave him his start by producing and promoting his first record.

In order to produce and promote The Four Freshman concert I needed money I didn't have, so I went looking for partners. I had remained friends with Arty and Jimmy Volpe, who ran the slot machines at my father's Italian Club so many years ago. By then they owned a small club on Route 30 in North Huntingdon where I would drop in to talk any time I was in the area. I called them up to pitch the Four Freshman show to them and they liked it. They went in for a third of the deal.

My YSU roommate, Monk Molinari, went in for a third, and that left me with a third. Monk was a good partner. I could count on him to come up with the money we needed to pay for the upfront expenses, and the Volpe's coughed up with their share, as well.

The night of the concert arrived and I hadn't sold enough seats to break even. I needed a walk-up crowd to put me over the top. Unfortunately, in spite of the support and attendance of friends and family who drove in from Trafford and Pittsburgh and bought tickets for the show, I didn't get what I needed. But the show went on, nevertheless.

To start their performance The Four Freshman just walked out on the stage with no introduction. I didn't know enough to emcee the show myself. There was a lot I didn't know. This would be the first and only concert I was ever to promote during which I actually sat in the audience and watched the show. When the Four Freshmen strolled out on the Stambaugh stage unannounced, the audience was delighted. They looked fantastic when the spotlights hit them and even though I knew I was losing on the deal, it was exhilarating. It was *my show*.

At one point in their performance the leader of the group announced, "Ladies and gentlemen we want to thank Pat DiCesare for presenting tonight's show." The audience applauded and I felt so proud. To hear my name spoken from the stage as the man who was putting on the show excited me, to say the least.

But I didn't even think about going back stage after the show to meet the singers. I didn't want pictures or autographs. I didn't want the attention. Tim Tormey had taught me, "This is a business so treat it as a business. To you, the act is your product, they are not stars. Just take care of your business, let the act take care of its business, get the show on and over with, get you're your money, and move on to the next show."

The Four Freshman put on a great show. The audience loved it, but more importantly to me, Dr. Chuey loved it. When I did the final accounting, our partnership lost $900. Monk gave me his $300 share, the Volpe's gave me theirs, and I went to the Friendly Loan Company to borrow mine. It was my first Pat DiCesare Production and the real start of my career. I lost money on it but I was not discouraged. I loved showbiz. There is no way to explain the feeling you get when the house lights go down, the drum roll starts, and the announcer shouts out, "Ladies and gentlemen, Pat DiCesare presents..." The music begins, the crowd cheers and whistles, the curtain opens and the act stands in the spotlight. It's show time!

I loved that feeling and knew I wanted—no, I *needed—* more.

Regal Records

In September of 1963 I was ready to start another year at Youngstown University. I had applied to several law schools hoping I would be accepted during my senior year of undergraduate work. However, my life changed drastically the day I got a phone call from Tim Tormey asking me to come to his office in Pittsburgh to talk about a proposal he had for me.

I liked going to the Carlton House. Everyone in the Pittsburgh music business hung out there. So I drove to Pittsburgh and when I arrived at Tim's office and walked in the door I found myself face-to-face with one of the most attractive, well built, well dressed girls I had ever seen. She could have been a model, a singer, or an actress. She was a knockout. The college girls at YSU sure didn't look like this girl! I tried to act as cool as possible and in my deepest voice said to her, "My name is Pat DiCesare and I'm here to see Tim. He's expecting me."

"Are you related to Mike DiCesare?" she asked.

"He's my brother. Do you know him?"

"We went to Edinboro together," she replied. "We called him 'the bear.'"

"That's him." I said. She told me her name was Tammy and that she had been a freshman at Edinoro College when Mike was a senior. Edinboro had only 400 students, and they all knew Mike.

After a bit of this pleasant chit-chat, Tim called me into his office. He told me that he, Nick Cenci, and Herbie Cohen were starting a new distributorship called Regal Records, on Fifth Avenue in Pittsburgh. They wanted me to manage their startup company for a salary of $500 a week. That was an enormous amount of money at the time. I didn't even give it a second thought. "Yes, I'll do it." I needed the money because I had been accepted to Dickinson School of Law in Carlisle, PA after my graduation from Youngstown State.

But I could only work for Tim for one semester, I told him. I would have to resume my studies at Youngstown State in January 1964.

Regal Records was located on Fifth Avenue near Pride Street where the Del Vikings producer Joe Averbach had his office. *It would be great,* I thought, *to work with guys who made and promoted records again and to get paid $500 a week for it. That was astronomical!*

Nick Cenci came by to go over the floor design for my office and warehouse and plan the opening, but I didn't like most of his ideas much—I had ideas of my own. I deferred to his advice, though, because he was one of the best record guys in the country and I felt fortunate to be working with him.

Herbie Cohen provided me with an assistant—Judy. She was attractive, well-built girl from Herbie's Fenway Record Distributors. All the girls I'd met in the record business were good looking, but, Judy was also quite capable and I thought that she could be my successor when I returned to school. Herbie and Nick had an office about two blocks down the street and in fact, most of Pittsburgh's record businesses were located in the same area.

Nick Cenci

One of the best record guys to come out of the City of Pittsburgh was Nick Cenci. He could get new records played nationally and turn them into hits just by getting them started in Pittsburgh. Nick was also a hit producer himself.

In January of 1962 Tim Tormey left the record distribution business and opened Artists Producers. Tim no longer wanted to work for someone else. He wanted to focus his attention on promoting concerts, managing recording artists, and running a night club.

Not long after opening his new business, a kid named Luigi Sacco walked into his office. Luigi wanted to make it in the entertainment business as a singer and songwriter. Tim called Nick Cenci and told him Luigi might be worth a listen. Nick asked Luigi to come over to his office on Fifth Avenue. Luigi hailed from Beaver County, Pennsylvania and he brought a female songwriter with him by the name of Twyla Herbert. They auditioned for Nick in the office and Nick liked their material. At the time, the Four Seasons were a big national singing group on the strength of Frankie Valli's unique falsetto and Nick felt that Luigi had a similar appeal.

He asked Luigi and Twyla to go back home to practice and suggested a few changes to Nick in the way he sang Twyla's songs, specifically that he emulate Frankie Valli's sound as closely as possible, especially on the Four Seasons hit, "Sherry." They followed his instructions and when they returned, Nick, who had great ears for hit music, was knocked out.

Nick had spent some time in recording studios and wanted to produce records. Although he was not a musician and couldn't read music, he understood the makings of a hit. He had started out in the mid-fifties as Jay Michael's boy. Jay was the big jock in town at WCAE Radio and Nick had started working for him right out of high school. Getting into the record business as a promoter was a natural for Nick. He had Jay in his corner and Jay was willing to play any record Nick thought was a hit.

A few years later, Nick moved into the big leagues with Mercury Records. He met Herbie Cohen, an up-and-coming Pittsburgh distributor. As a promoter who could get records played when other promoters couldn't, Nick earned Herbie's respect and confidence.

Nick helped Herbie get into record production and they set up their own label and publishing company. They approached the celebrated Pittsburgh DJ, Porky Chedwick, with an idea. Porky was quite an unusual DJ—a white jock at an all-black station. Porky hosted an on-air program he called "Dusty Discs," playing old records no other radio stations had ever played. Nick, Tim and Herbie obtained the rights to the masters of these recordings from the original labels, put them on one LP, and sold them as Dusty Discs Volume 1. It sold over 3,000 copies the first day, so they quickly compiled Volume 2. Their company was making good money from these LP's and so was Porky Chedwick.

Porky convinced record company owners to give him the original masters of these recordings at no charge. Guys like George Goldner from Gone Records and Jerry Wexler from Atlantic Records were happy to help Porky because they knew they could depend on him to play their new releases. It was a veiled form of payola.

While I was attending Youngstown State in 1961 and also working for Tim Tormey three days a week, The Civic Arena in Pittsburgh was opened and the next year, Tim and Nick got Porky to call all the recording artists he had helped over the years by playing their records and ask them to come to Pittsburgh for the Civic Arena's first rock and roll concert. That was yet another form of payola in that the artists would play for little or no money, knowing that Porky would play their next new release.

The show was called "Porky Chedwick's Groove Spectacular." It featured twenty-four artists with Jackie Wilson as the headliner. Pittsburgh's Bobby Vinton had a number one hit at the time with "Roses Are Red" and his orchestra was tapped to back up all the other acts on the show. Bobby lobbied Tim to be billed as the top star and close the show. Tim explained to Bobby that he was out of his element playing in an all rhythm-and-blues show, but did agree to put Bobby on just before Jackie Wilson. With twenty-four artists on the bill the show ran so long the spotlight operators sent word to Tim the carbon arcs in the spotlights only had fifteen more minutes of life left and then there would no more spotlights on the stage. Tim was forced to cut a few scheduled acts, including Bobby Vinton. Bobby never forgave him for it.

The sellout show marked the beginning of Tim's concert promotion career and the end of his record distribution business. Nick and Herbie remained in the record business. Tim called his business Artist Producers because in addition to promoting concerts he intended to manage recording artists.

Lou Christie

One of those artists was Luigi Sacco, who brought to him his new version of the Twyla Herbert's song, "The Gypsy Cried." He sung it in a falsetto voice just the way Nick wanted it and it sounded very much like The Four Seasons hit, "Sherry." Nick took him into the studio and recorded the song with a full band and then took the tape to KQV, the top radio station in town, and got the program director to put it on rotation the next week, which meant it would get immediate airplay. He then had a sufficient number of 45's pressed for distribution and readied the record for release. But Luigi Sacco was not a name he could promote, so he called Luigi into his office and told him, "Luigi, your record is at the pressing plant now and you are no longer Luigi Sacco. From now on, your name is Lou Christie."

"Lou Christie!?" Luigi exclaimed. "How did you come up with that?"

"I was reading *Billboard Magazine* and saw that someone named June Christy had a hit and I liked her name. You should be calling yourself Lou anyway, not Luigi. At least I kept that for you. Yeah, Lou Christie sounds good."

Luigi went along with it, but he hated the name. "I was pissed off about it for twenty years," he later said. "I wanted to keep my name and be a one-name performer, simply Lugee." But thanks to Nick Cenci, Lou Christie he had become.

Nick and Herbie immediately launched a record company they called Co & Ce Records and signed the rechristened Lou Christie to the label. Because Nick was a great record promoter, he convinced not only KQV but many other stations around the country to put the as-yet unproven record in heavy rotation and the result was an overnight hit wherever it was played.

One of the labels Herbie and Nick distributed was Roulette Records in New York, owned by the infamous Morris Levy, who was reputed to be heavily connected to the Mafia. He was a man you did not cross in any way. Nick and Herbie made a deal with Morris to distribute the record nationwide. Lou

Christie was now a Roulette Records recording artist and his record, "The Gypsy Cried" was released nationally, reaching #24 on the Billboard charts. It was the first of many Nick Cenci-produced hits to come.

Greetings from the U.S. Army

By January 1964 we were doing so well with Regal Records that Tim, Herbie, and Nick offered me more than $500 a week to stay for another semester and I agreed. The Vietnam War was escalating and more and more guys were getting drafted. To avoid the draft you had to be married and have a child or be a registered college student. If you were a student you had to apply for a student deferment at the start of each new semester. As I did not return to Youngstown State, I didn't file the application. The next thing I knew, I got a "greetings" letter from Uncle Sam.

I reported for the required physical exam and to my surprise and dismay, passed! I expected to fail the physical because I had applied two years in a row years to the Marine ROTC program and failed their physical each time. With my eyesight and allergies, they assured me, I would never pass an Army physical. So I assumed that I would never be drafted. But apparently, the Army was passing anyone who could breathe.

Feeling depressed the next day I went into work at Regal Records. When I told Jack Hakim and Nick Cenci that I passed the physical they couldn't believe it either. Nick immediately called his friend Captain Danzelli, who was in charge of a National Guard unit at the Hunt Armory in Pittsburgh.

Then they quickly gathered 25 LP records of top-selling artists like Frank Sinatra, Dean Martin and Johnny Mathis because that was Captain Danzelli's type of music. The three of us drove together to the Hunt Armory to see the Captain and Nick laid our box of 25 LP's on the desk in front of him.

"What's this?" He asked.

"These are for you to enjoy," Nick responded. "Pat needs to get into the National Guard, now. He just passed his physical for the Army and he is going to be sworn in and leave for active duty this week if he doesn't. Can you get him in?"

"That's a tall order. We'll have to act fast, but I can do it." He picked up the phone and made a call. "Doctor," we heard him say, "I need a physical done immediately. Can we come over now?" He drove us to a doctor's office, where I was administered yet another physical and again I passed. Captain Danzelli then said to me, "Raise your right hand," and he swore me in on the spot. I was now a member of the Pennsylvania National Guard.

This was important because being in the National Guard meant that I had to serve only six months of active duty and another 5 ½ years in the active reserves. Had I been drafted into the Army, I would have had to spend two years on active duty and 4 years in active reserves. I probably would have been shipped off to Vietnam. As it was, I had to attend two meetings in the evenings and a serve a full weekend once a month at the Armory in Pittsburgh until I got called to active duty for six months of training. Joining the National Guard had a profound impact on my life, but at least I still had my life.

Chapter Nine

Three Rivers Stadium

Alice Cooper and Hurricane Agnes (June-July 1972)

The Summer of 1972 marked the beginning of stadium rock concerts as we know and love them today. One of the ground breaking concerts nationally that helped to bring stadium rock into the mainstream was my Alice Cooper concert at Three Rivers Stadium in Pittsburgh on July 11, 1972.

The first major stadium show ever was The Beatles first performance before 55,000 screaming fans at Shea Stadium in New York City on August 15, 1965. It was technically primitive, with inadequate sound and staging, but it was the biggest-grossing concert in history.

It would take another six years before stadium concerts began to come into their own, and the problems I had to solve with the Alice Cooper show were to become standard operating procedure for promoters across the country for decades to come.

As 1972 began, the summer was shaping up to be a blockbuster concert season. Some of the hit acts and shows that I had planned included Englebert Humperdink, Rod Stewart, Chicago, The Jackson Five, The Rolling Stones, Emerson Lake and Palmer, Sonny and Cher, Deep Purple and the Broadway musical, *Jesus Christ Superstar*.

The shock-rock band Alice Cooper was one of the hottest acts in the country at that time, with huge hits like "School's Out." Alice Cooper's manager, Shep Gordon, called and asked me to promote the band that summer as a stadium act. I had promoted my first ballpark concert at Three Rivers Stadium the previous summer with Three Dog Night and sold 30,000 tickets. An Alice Cooper show would be much more elaborate and demanding and it would, of necessity, take stadium concerts to a whole new level. The challenge from a sales standpoint would be to secure the best possible support talent to make it a dynamite experience for the fans and also to attract 40,000 of them.

It was a huge risk, but I accepted Shep's offer and agreed to promote the show. Terry Bassett from Concerts West then approached me about promoting another Three Dog Night show at the stadium that summer, and since we had done well with them once already, I agreed to that one as well. So suddenly, we had not one, but two upcoming stadium concerts to promote and I wondered—*could the City of Pittsburgh support two stadium shows in one summer? Were there that many entertainment dollars available in the area?*

Pittsburgh historically was not a good summer concert city. The Civic Arena, the only venue hosting big shows at this time, had an expensive retractable roof primarily for presenting summer performances, but I never believed that it was particularly helpful in selling tickets. Summer months were—for many people—for outdoor activities, not indoor concerts.

Pittsburgh, we always thought, could support maybe four major rock shows a year, but now I was considering more than that this summer. It was a scary thought, but I was convinced they all had great potential.

Jesus Christ Superstar was a particularly exciting prospect. I had already sold out a week-long run at Heinz Hall with 2,500 seats and then played two sold-out dates at the Civic Arena in 1971. Its composer, Andrew Lloyd Weber, must have thought a lot of us because he chose Pittsburgh as the first arena date for the 1972 national tour. I loved the show and was excited about doing it again, although everyone else thought I was crazy. But I went full steam ahead anyway.

It was that first stadium show with Alice Cooper, though, that was the biggest risk and the biggest hurdle. Other promoters had made two dismal attempts to mount concerts at Three Rivers Stadium. The first, with trumpeter Al Hirt, sold only 5,000 tickets, and the second, with Aretha Franklin did even worse. The stages were small and the sound was poor. The setup for Alice Cooper would have to be light years ahead of those shows.

Terry Bassett had some ambitious idea for Three Dog Night. He wanted the band to do ten stadium shows that summer and erect four 14-foot TV screens at each one so that every member of the audience, regardless of their seating, would have a close-up view of the performers. Their big problem was they didn't know how or where to put up a stage or how to build a roof outdoors to protect the band in the event of rain.

Before Three Dog Night, though, Alice Cooper would be our test. I thought Alice could draw the 30,000 that Three Dog Night drew, but I wanted to eclipse that concert attendance record and to do that I would have to add a few strong opening acts. I wanted to produce the greatest rock concert that Pittsburgh had ever seen.

Three Rivers' management was of little help. Other than the three aforementioned shows, they had no real rock concert experience. I had to talk them into it. When I showed them the kind of numbers that T-shirt sales, beer and other concessions, and parking fees would generate, they were convinced.

The Pittsburgh Pirates management was not so easy to convince. They made it clear they did not want rock concerts at their stadium; especially not an act like Alice Cooper, because they thought the audience would ruin their playing field. I would have to schedule any show I did there during an away stretch, when the Pirates were on the road for at least four days. I would need a day or two before the show to set up the stage and convert the facility from a baseball field to a concert venue, and then I would need a day after the show to tear down.

Though the Pirates objected, the stadium's other principle tenant, the Steelers, voiced no such concerns. Their publicity director, Joe Gordon, was a good friend of mine, and since our shows would be scheduled long before the start of football season, our shows didn't bother him.

As I continued to meet with Pirates management to iron out an agreement I became aware they weren't the problem; it was the stadium grounds crew. Those guys had a strong union and if you wanted to make anything happen at the stadium, you needed their blessing.

I had attended many Pirate games and I had season tickets for the Steelers, but as many games as I had seen, I had never paid the slightest attention to the grounds crew. The leader of the crew was Dirt DiNardo. It took me a while to figure out that while talking with management, management was talking to the Dirt. He was The Man at Three Rivers Stadium.

Besides convincing Pirates management I had other questions to answer. Shep Gordon wanted to know how I was going to protect the acts onstage in the event of rain. He wanted to know what I was going to *use* for a stage. The Pirates wouldn't allow me to erect anything on the field that could cause damage or penetrate the ground in any way. I could dig no holes for support. How was I to build a stage and a roof without support? Where would I find a sound system that could cover an entire stadium? I had no idea, but I assured Shep that I had all the answers.

There were other problems, as well. I would have to erect the stage, towers for the roof as well as the roof itself, risers for spotlights in the seating areas, rig overhead lights above the stage, provide a temporary office behind the stage as well as dressing rooms there also. I would need barriers to prevent the crowd from getting too close or behind the stage. I had to protect the acts. I had to contain the fans in their seats and prevent them for stampeding onto the field. In addition, I would have to get a huge amount of electrical power to the stage and other points of use. None of this was available at the stadium, or anywhere else, for that matter, and as we started planning for the show, we discovered there was no source for it anywhere else, either.

At this time, I was planning to build a home on a 120 acre plot of farmland outside Pittsburgh that I owned with my older brother Ralph, who was a masonry contractor. He was building a house for a client, which was on my way home.

I stopped at the construction site one evening to find Ralph and his crew laying bricks on the third story of a gigantic home. He looked down from the scaffolding and shouted, "What's up little brother?"

"I just wanted to go over the plans for my house. I thought since you were out this way we could talk," I said.

"I can't stop right now. I have to get this house bricked today. Come on up." That was my brother. He was the hardest worker I had ever known and he was a perfectionist. He never wanted to stop working even to eat lunch, let alone to talk to his brother.

I peered up at the scaffold and thought better of it, "Maybe I'll just come over to your house when you aren't busy. I'll see you later." Sitting in my car, I looked at the scaffolding he was working on. He must have been working 35 feet high. Suddenly, inspiration hit. "That's the roof over my stage!" I thought.

At home that night I drew up a rough plan of my idea. I called Ralph and told him about the concert I was planning at Three Rivers Stadium. "Do you think you could build me six piers of scaffolding around a stage about as high as you built the scaffolding on that house you were bricking today?" I asked. "I want to build three piers on each side of a stage and connect the tops of the piers with 4 inch angle irons. I want to stretch a fabric from one side to the other about thirty feet above the stage. The stage will probably be 40 feet by 40 feet.

Do you think you could build these piers and the stage from the scaffolding that you have?"

"I don't know. How long will my scaffolding be tied up?"

"Probably a week."

"I couldn't tie my equipment up that long, Pat. Call Safeway Scaffolding in Pittsburgh. They can rent it to you." He suggested. "Tell me though, how are you going to anchor all of this? If you don't anchor the scaffolding properly the tops can tip inward and collapse on top of your stage. You have to tie all of this to something."

"They won't let me dig any holes or drive anything into the field."

"That's going to be tough. I suppose that you could fill 55 gallon barrels with water and tie off the scaffolding to that and attach the bottom portion of the piers to the stage. What are you going to use as the fabric for the roof?"

"I don't know yet. Do you have any idea?"

"Visquene."

"What's Visquene?"

"Sheets of heavy plastic. We use them when we want to keep snow out of our foundations during the winter. You're going to need ten times more scaffolding than I have to pull this off and you're going to need a pretty big rig to erect it. Who is going to help you?"

"I don't know. I was hoping—you."

"I don't think you realize what a big undertaking this is. It's a dangerous job. You need guys to work 30 or 40 feet in the air. It's going to be tough to find guys to do that kind of work.

"Ralph, what happens to the Visquene if it rains during a show?"

"That's a problem. You not only have to worry about rain but also wind. If you get a strong wind and the stage and roof is tied together, the Visquene roof can act as a sail and it could lift the stage right up in the air."

"What can I do?"

"Two things—pray it doesn't rain and find yourself an architect or an engineer-right now. Talk to an architect before you get yourself in trouble. Frankly, I think you should forget the whole idea, brother. Take your show to the Arena where you don't have these worries."

I loved the challenge of being the first to promote a major rock concert at Three Rivers Stadium. Yes, I had problems to solve, but I always had problems to solve. I had never let that stop me and I wouldn't let it stop me now.

For the sound system I turned to my friends from Lititz, Pennsylvania, Roy and Gene Clair. They had pioneered large concert sound and I remembered them telling me the future of rock concerts was in stadiums, and now it was clear they were right. For lighting, I called Bob Miller from Flexitrol Lighting in Pittsburgh. He assured me he could handle the task. Like Shep Gordon, both the Clair Brothers and Bob Miller wanted to know what I was going to use for a stage and a roof.

"I'm working on that," I told them.

That night, as I was driving from my office to my home, I stopped for a traffic light at a busy intersection. A large trailer truck pulled up alongside of me and after the light changed I could see that it was pulling a very long flatbed trailer. Again, inspiration struck. "That's my stage!" I thought.

I estimated the trailer to be about 40 feet long, 8 feet wide, and 5 feet high. If I were to put five of those flatbeds together side-by-side I would have a 40 foot x 40 foot stage—perfect for a stadium show. The tires could straddle the pitcher's mound so we wouldn't have to drive anything into the ground.

I remembered Tim Tormey telling me about a good buddy who owned a fleet of trucks by the name of Bob Eazor. I called Tim in California and he told he would have Bob call me. A few minutes later, he did, "Tim told me about this crazy idea of yours, Pat. I've been in the trucking business for a long time but I've never used a truck for a stage before. Tell me what you need."

I gave him all of the details and he could not have been more helpful. "My drivers are Teamsters," he explained. "Will that be a problem?"

"Bob, the ushers, the ticket takers and the sellers, the people who clean restrooms, the guys who take care of the field and unload the trucks, the electricians, the stagehands—they are all union workers. What's one more?"

He agreed to provide the trailers I needed.

Then I asked him the big question: "How much will all of this cost me?"

"Nothing. Tim tells me you're a good guy! How about a few tickets to the show for the drivers and their kids?"

"Deal!"

That left the roof problem to resolve. It could get quite windy in that stadium. Ralph was right. I needed professional help. I happened to know that one of my neighbors was an architect. I went to his home and knocked on his door to introduce myself. He was intrigued and agreed to help.

The following week he presented me with an elaborate blueprint that included five flatbed trailers and three thirty-foot towers of scaffolding on each side of the stage. They would be connected by angle irons with half-inch holes which would allow airplane hangar wire to be threaded through and spread 30 feet high across the stage to the opposite angle iron. The Visquene would then be spread over the hangar wire and tied down. As we could not drive anything into the field to anchor the roof down, we would use Ralph's idea and fill 50 gallon drums with water and tie them to the scaffolding towers.

"The only thing you have to worry about is heavy wind and rain," The architect said. "If it rains hard and the wind starts blowing during the concert, have a few guys climb the towers, untie the Visquene, and let it blow away or it might carry your stage away into the air."

"How strong would the wind have to blow to do that?"

"I don't know, but I do know of a circus tent that blew away in a 60 miles per hour wind."

So what are the odds, I thought, *of a 60 MPH wind during my show?* I did a little research and found that Pittsburgh gets rain, on the average of only 90 days a year. The odds were one in four. So, as I so often did, I gambled.

Calling Shep Gordon, I proudly announced, "The stage and roof problems are solved."

Alice Cooper was a strong draw. I had sold out the Civic Arena with him, but that was only 15,000 seats. At Three Rivers Stadium we would have to nearly triple that so I had to choose the support acts carefully. After checking with all the agents I worked with and doing a little research I selected two British bands with albums on the charts: Uriah Heep and Humble Pie. I thought more of the latter's guitar player than I did of the band. The girls loved Peter Frampton. I thought at the time that Frampton could be a bigger star on his own than he would ever be with Humble Pie.

Figuring on 40,000 seats, I calculated if priced the tickets at $4.75, $5.75 and $6.75, depending on the seat locations, I could gross about $240,000. I had never grossed that much in ticket sales at a single concert before. The three acts would get 60% of the ticket sales, or about $140,000. At first I thought I would pay the stadium the standard 10% of the gross sales, or $24,000, but then I figured they would make a fortune on food and t-shirt concessions, so I decided to offer a flat $10,000 and let them keep all the ancillary profits.

With these numbers I would earn my biggest single payday ever—$50,000. I never even dreamed that was possible when I started out. Now, it became all I could think about. The thought obsessed me!

All three acts accepted my deal. We set the date for June 23. Shep Gordon insisted that because Alice was the headliner he should not only close the show, but he would also be the only act to perform after sundown, the only act to perform with the benefit of stage lighting. I accepted his terms.

In April, I finally settled things with the Pirates and obtained a lease with Three Rivers Stadium. I secured contracts with all three acts and because my reputation with the agents for always paying their acts was solid I didn't have to pay the usual fifty percent deposit. The date was on! There was no turning back. It would be largest rock concert in the history of Pittsburgh, and possibly the largest stadium concert since The Beatles at Shea Stadium.

With Shep Gordon's agreement, I put an ad in newspapers that Sunday announcing the concert, had KQV run teasers on the air, and put tickets on sale the next day. The Pirates were scheduled to play the Dodgers on June 21. That didn't leave much time for setting up the stage and roof. But it had to be done, and do it we would.

Thursday, June 22: The Beginning: 12:01 A.M.

At just past midnight on the morning of June 22nd five flatbed trucks arrived at the centerfield gate. I was already in my temporary office, located near the pitcher's mound. As I walked outside to greet the drivers I felt a few scattered raindrops, but it didn't overly concern me. My plan was to have the stadium converted from a baseball stadium to a concert venue in just 36 hours. I had to have it ready for the sound check by noon Friday.

Back in my office, Jimmy Vaccaro walked in, drying his face, and said, "I don't like this rain. It's going to be hard to keep these guys working out there."

"How bad is it now?" I asked.

"It's light, but steady…just enough to be aggravating. The head of the grounds crew is being a real pain in the ass. He wants to talk to you. He says it's important."

"Tell him to come over. I'll talk to him. What does he want anyway?"

"I don't know exactly, but all he does is complain. He and his guys haven't done a thing but bitch. I think you better talk to him."

"Okay. Tell him to come talk to me. What's his name?"

They call him Dirt and he told me if you want to talk to him you have to come to him outside in the rain, like everyone else."

"Then tell him to go screw himself! Who the hell does he think he is? I'm the guy that's paying the bills here."

"Hey, don't take it out on me! This isn't like the Civic Arena or the Syria Mosque. These are union guys. They don't want to work. They're pissed because they're working a rock show in the rain."

Storming out of the office, I followed Jimmy to the dugout, where a group of workers were standing around drinking coffee.

Dirt greeted me with a sly smile. "Pat, what do you think about working in the rain?"

Irritated with him, I shot back, "The Pirates play in the rain, don't they? The Steelers don't call the game when it snows. You work for them and right now you're working for us. The show must go on. This is going to blow over anyway."

"Yeah, but this is a baseball and a football stadium. There shouldn't be rock shows here. Your people are just going to ruin this place. They're going to tear it up. You'll see."

"Look, I'm on a tight schedule. I need to get this stage and roof built by 8:00 tomorrow morning. The barrier has to be set up by noon. This is my assistant, Jimmy Vaccaro. He will tell you what we need. Now I have other work to do."

"Vaccaro!" he exclaimed. So you're both Italian. Me, too. Well if you're Italian, you know good food. You know lasagna, hot sausage, provolone, salami. If you want us to work we have to eat. So what are you going to feed us?"

Dirt was really starting to piss me off. But the reality of the situation was that I could not afford to piss *him* off.

"I tell you what," I told him, "You are Italian and we are Italian so we will feed you. Jimmy, call my brother Joe right now and tell him to have my Dad cook some lasagna, hot sausage, and meatballs for these guys. Have him bring salami, some provolone, olives, and that good Italian bread at DeLallo's. We're going to feed Dirt and crew."

"But Pat, it's 1:00 in the morning," he moaned.

"I know what time it is. Wake him up. Have him here by 6:00 in the morning."

That seemed to satisfy Dirt, for the moment.

Thursday, June 22: 6:00 A.M.

At 6:00 in the morning Jimmy was back in my office. "Your brothers and your Dad have set up the food in the catering area," he informed me. "The workers are taking a break now. Do you want something to eat?"

"No. You go ahead. I'll get something later. I want to call the weather guy at Channel 11. He promised to keep me posted on the rain."

I'd been awake for 24 hours by then. I was too excited to sleep and there was too much to do anyway. I had Jimmy bring me coffee and mentally prepared myself for the long day ahead. Sleep would have to wait until tonight...if then.

The flatbeds were followed by Safeway Scaffolding's trucks carrying the scaffolding to build the towers. The flatbed drivers did an excellent job of placing them as close together as we needed and at the exact spot we had chosen over the pitcher's mound. Bob Eazor was a real gentleman. He sent his newest trucks. Still, we would have to cover the beds with plywood painted black to make the stage floor smooth and even.

Building the six towers 30 to 40 feet high was a formidable task. My architects found four Native Americans who had no fear of height and were willing to do the work. In addition to building the stage and roof and tying it all together, we had to construct a four foot high barrier across the front of the stage and construct two elevated work stations in the seating area behind the batter's box for the sound mixer and lighting director. Then, we had to run massive electric cabling from the work stations to the stage. It took a total of 36 workers on the various crews to pull off this massive effort.

As the sun was rising, just when I thought everything was under control, Jimmy Vaccaro came rushing back in to the office.

"We've got problems. Big problems!" he exclaimed. "The job's shut down. Nobody's working."

"Which job shut down? What the hell are you talking about?"

"Nobody's working out there! The union won't let them. The union shut the job down."

"Which union?"

"It's Dirt! It's that Dirt guy."

Again, I rushed out to confront Dirt. "Dirt. What the hell is going on? Why aren't you guys working?" I yelled.

"You've got other union guys doing *my* guys' work. So I shut the job down."

"Dirt, last night it was the rain. This morning it was lasagna. Now we have other unions doing your unions' work. How do we fix this problem?"

"This isn't the Civic Arena. This is Three Rivers Stadium. We are in charge of this field. You have to go through us if you want to do anything. Capice? You're not in charge. We are."

Who is this character? I thought. *Is he mentally ill?* A $50,000 payday was on the line and all I had to do was stay calm and get the job done. So very calmly I responded,

"Okay, Dirt. You're in charge. What do you need?"

"Well for one thing, those guys building the towers have to leave. We will build that."

"Okay, Dirt, but do you really want your guys working 40 feet in the air in this rain? Our guys are Indians. They're ironworkers. This is what they do. They walk on the tops of bridges. Are you sure you want your guys to do that?"

"Wait here, I'll be back," he said.

A few minutes later he was back, out of breath, black saliva flowing from one corner of his mouth from chewing tobacco. After wiping his mouth with the palm of his hand, he extended his hand and said, "Go ahead and let those Indians do the work. Let's shake on it."

Another problem solved. But many more were yet to come.

Thursday, June 22: 5:00 P.M.

Throughout the entire day I continued to deal with one crisis after another. The city demanded we hire one hundred cops before they would grant us a permit. Complications cropped up in erecting the lighting towers. The unions kept howling. It was one thing after another.

But the worst problem—the one problem I had no power to solve—was the continuing rain. My niece, Denise, was in the office with me when the phone rang. She took the call, listened for a minute with a shocked look on her face, then hung up with barely a word. Looking at me she gave me the bad news. "That was the weatherman from Channel 11 returning your call. There's a storm off the Atlantic coast called Hurricane Agnes and it might be heading this way."

"Oh my God! This is all I need!"

Then things got even worse. One of the architects in charge of erecting the roof came into my office walked in, looking grim. "This rain is coming down too hard to put the roof up," he told me. "I don't like this whole thing. It's too dangerous. Maybe you should cancel the show."

"What? I can't cancel now! It's too late. I'll lose a fortune. Don't you ever let anyone hear you say those words."

"Look Pat, it's dangerous out there. What if the towers get hit by lightning? We can't fight this rain and you can't do this show. We're quitting."

I called Jimmy to the office and gave him the bad news. "Channel 11 says there's a hurricane coming and the architects quit on us."

The news that a hurricane might be on its way must have been too much for him. All he said was "They quit? Who is going to supervise the roof construction?"

"You're looking at him. You go get some sleep and take our crew with you. Tell the stagehands they can come in about 8 in the morning to set the light trusses on the towers. They should be built by then. They can set the spots up and everyone should be ready for the sound check by noon as planned."

"I don't know. You might be too optimistic about that. Did you see all of that scaffolding out there? You only have four people putting it up."

"I know. But it will get done. Now get going and get some sleep."

Walking out onto the field, I waded through puddles of water towards home plate. As the rain pounded my face, I saw that all the workers had left the field to get some well-deserved sleep. All was quiet and there was no one in sight but me. It was an eerie feeling. At that moment I felt helpless, frightened, and alone.

Thursday, June 22: 8:00 P.M.

The concert was scheduled to begin in less than 24 hours. I'd been in this position many times, but I had never such strong feelings of uncertainty before. I was beginning to doubt that this show would go on. It was the dreaded rain. *What could I do about a damn hurricane if it came our way? Would the roof hold the water? Would the towers cave in? Would the wind carry the stage away? Would somebody get electrocuted? What the hell am I doing here???*

I turned around and saw my accountant, Francis, standing next to me. "I've been trying to call you," he said.

"I haven't been in the office for a while."

"I got it! I got the permit and you don't have to hire a hundred cops. They settled for forty."

"That's great, Francis. Good job." That was one small piece of good news I needed. I didn't tell him that we may have to cancel the show if the rain didn't let up. I didn't tell him about Hurricane Agnes.

Excusing myself, I walked back into my office, put my head down on the desk to rest for a minute, and then fell asleep.

Friday, June 23: 12-something A.M.

I felt someone shaking me on the shoulder and I awoke. It was one of the four Indians who were building the towers. He informed me they had built the scaffolding three sections high and now they had to get the scaffolding in the air. "We need the forklift," he said.

Dirt's crew was gone and wouldn't be back until morning. I knew that if I had anyone else operate the forklift Dirt would stop the job again. The forklift was on the side of the stage with the keys in it. I figured what the hell, I rented it, I can use it. What Dirt didn't know wouldn't hurt him. I motioned the Indian to sit in it and drive. I was using my hands to communicate, thinking they didn't speak English for some reason, then I said, "Can you operate it?"

"Of course I can"

One more problem solved

Friday, June 23: 6:00 A.M.

Jimmy was back and he was frantic. "You should see it out there, Pat. The wharf is flooded. The Point is flooded. There's water everywhere. All three rivers are rising. The water is almost touching the bottom of the bridges. I've never seen that happen before. It's scary. I wonder if anyone will even be able get here for the show."

"Well, Alice Cooper will be here!" I responded, trying to calm Jimmy down. "Shep just called. Their plane gets in at 10:00 and I have a limo picking them up. The Indians got the roof up. We're ready. All we need is the bands to get here with their equipment. Find out what time everyone's equipment is set to arrive."

At 10:30 a.m. Shep and the band checked into the Hilton downtown and he called me to come over and meet them there. It was raining so hard on the way the windshield wipers could barely keep up. I buzzed Shep from the lobby and went up to his suite. Greeting me with a big hug his first words were, "Are we going to have a show tonight?"

Alice was sprawled out on an oversized stuffed chair with a beer in his hand. "Hey, man, how was the flight?" I asked him.

"Sit down and have a beer with me."

Shep said, "Bring me up to date. What's going on? What are the other acts saying?"

"I talked to both acts last night. They heard all about Hurricane Agnes and they wanted to wait as long as possible before they made any moves," I answered as Alice opened a beer and handed it to me.

The room phone rang. Shep answered and then handed the phone to me. "It's for you. It's someone with the stadium."

It was the stadium manager. "Pat," he said, "the water is starting to come up to the stadium wall at center field. The Channel 11 weatherman says there's no letup in sight. It will get worse. If the water gets close to the power room we'll have to shut it down, but for now the show is still on. I'll keep you posted."

I relayed the message to Shep. Alice just opened another beer and handed it to me, "Here, drink up!"

As I looked out of the window from the penthouse suite I could see the Fort Pitt Blockhouse at the point where the Ohio, Allegheny, and Monongahela rivers converged and where a major battle of the French and Indian War had once taken place. The fort was inundated.

Shep interrupted my thoughts. "Pat, do you like beer?"

"No. Not really." I said.

"I'm into scotch."

"I drink scotch when I drink, which isn't too often. I'm not much of a drinker." I said.

"No, I mean I'm into *investing* in scotch. Instead of buying stocks, we buy scotch as an investment. You should think about that." Alice joined in as we continued to discuss the merits of scotch as an investment. At first, it felt strange talking with Alice Cooper about investing, but I found him to be an intelligent and interesting conversationalist, a far cry from his stage persona at that time. He was a down to earth guy. I realized his show was all just an act, a gimmick!

11:00 a.m. Another call from the stadium manager. Water was now flowing onto center field. I passed the news on to Shep and Alice. They still didn't seem too concerned about the possibility of the show being cancelled. We drank more beer.

11:15 a.m. The phone rang again. Water was now pouring into the electrical room. The situation is too dangerous, said the stadium manager, we must cancel the show.

11:20 a.m. As I was beginning to tell Shep and Alice the bad news, the phone rang again. It was Jimmy Vaccaro. "Pat we're ready for the sound check. Where is everyone?"

"Tell Denise to call KQV and tell them the show is cancelled due to the flood," I told him "Have the jocks ask the people to hold on to their tickets until further notice. Make it clear that no one should come to the stadium today. I'm with Alice and Shep. We'll reschedule the date. Stop everything until you hear back from me."

Jimmy pleaded, "You can't cancel, Pat. You'll lose a fortune."

Jimmy was right, but that was all I could do.

I looked at Alice and shrugged. He said, "Here, have another beer."

I had no idea at that point how much money this cancellation would actually cost me, but I did know that my big $50,000 payday had just sunk underwater. But I couldn't dwell on that right then. I had to get Shep and Alice to reschedule the date—now!

So that's what I did. We settled on July 11th. I immediately called the stadium and that date was open. The Pirates were out of town. I called the agents for the other two acts to give them the bad news and the rain check date Shep and I had settled on.

Finally, I called Jimmy Vaccaro and told him to shut everything down at the stadium and send everyone home.

Showtime: July 11, 1972

After we announced the make-up date for the Alice Cooper show I was surprised and pleased that almost no one wanted a refund for the cancelled June 23rd show. It was still a sellout.

Our various crews were already familiar with the stage and roof set up at the stadium, so things went smoothly on that front. I did have a problem with one of the opening acts, though. I had to replace Uriah Heep with another act, and Humble Pie manager Dee Anthony was now promoting the band as simply Peter Frampton, not Humble Pie. Dee was a pugnacious bully. He delayed putting Frampton on the stage until well after 8:00 because he wanted his act to perform with the benefit of stage lighting, in spite of the contract. That sparked an unpleasant confrontation, but in the end it all worked out.

The audience loved the show and so did Shep. There was no rain and everything worked. It was, as I had hoped, Pittsburgh's biggest and most successful concert ever.

I wish I could say the same for it financially. I did not enjoy the $50,000 payday I had dreamed about. Nor did I *lose* as much as I thought I would. In fact, combining the June 23 losses with the July 11 profit, I broke even on the whole deal.

My old friend Jack Hooke once wisely told me, "Don't count your money until it's in the bank. Anything can happen." Considering everything, I was grateful for the break even outcome of my first major stadium show. There would be many more to come in the years ahead and most of them would make money...lots of money. I would eventually enjoy my $50,000 payday. And "stadium rock," which I am proud to have had a hand in creating, would become an international sensation.

I could have lost everything that night of June 23, 1972, but as it turned out, I lost nothing. And what I gained that night in wisdom and experience cannot be measured.

Chapter Ten
Tim Tormey and
Dick Clark, 1965

It was spring, 1965. Tim called to congratulate me. "Good job," he said, "I told you it was a winner." He was referring to the successful Dapper Dan Roundball Classic basketball game Sonny Vaccaro and I had created and promoted at the Civic Arena in March. The Roundball Classic pit the best high school senior players from Pennsylvania against the best in the United States, and it was a sellout.

"Thanks to you, Tim," I told him. "Without you it never would have happened,"

"What are you talking about? You're a promoter. That's what we do. We come up with ideas and we create events. That's what you and Sonny did. But, in any case, could you come by my office? I need to talk to you."

"Certainly, when?"

"Anytime. Just walk right up." His office was two floors above mine at the Carlton House.

My office consisted of a desk in a corner of someone else's office. It was a prestigious address, but I barely had room for a desk and a chair.

Entering Tim's office a few minutes later I saw his assistant and secretary, Tammy, looking better than ever. A few years later, Marlo Thomas would star on a hit TV series called *That Girl* and her character was very much like Tammy. Tammy was always well dressed in the latest fashion and she had the perfect body for it. She always made you think of spring.

"Hi, Tammy! How are you? You're looking great as usual. Is Tim on the phone?"

"Isn't he always?" she replied.

He was just hanging up as I walked in. "Patrick my boy, come in and sit down, I have some news you will be interested in. You know that I've been talking with Roz Ross from the William Morris Agency about putting together my own tours and calling them *The Shower of Stars*. Right now, I am in a bidding war against Dick Clark. Roz books all the acts for his *Caravan of Stars* tours. I want Gene Pitney as the headliner for my tour this summer, but when Roz told Dick about my show, Dick decided he wanted Gene as *his* headliner. Can you imagine that?"

I was impressed. "Wow, how did you pull Gene Pitney away from Dick? Doesn't everyone want to work for Dick Clark?"

"Well, Dick kept upping his offer and I kept upping my offer above his. Finally, Roz said 'Let's bring Gene Pitney to New York and have him sit down at the Park Sheraton with you in one room and Dick in another and you can both negotiate with him head-to-head until one of you has an agreement.'"

A few days later, that is precisely what they did. The bidding started at $3,500 a week, which was already at the top end of the scale at that time. Most single performers were lucky to get $1,000 a week. It went back and forth, with Gene going from room to room to room until Dick finally bid a whopping $5,000. That was more than Tim could handle.

But Tim had a trick up his sleeve. Instead of offering Pitney more money Tim told him "Here's what I'll do for you. I will call the show *Gene Pitney's Shower of Stars.*" Gene loved it. Tim knew that Dick's ego would never permit him to take his own name off his own show and he was right. It was an offer Dick would not match. So it was Tim who got Gene Pitney.

Dick Clark was upset, but he was also impressed. He told

Roz," I like this Tormey guy. Let's see if we can buy the whole show from him. Let him manage the tour and run it, but he'll work for me, and if I still like him, he can run the touring division of my company."

Tim had already sold all the available shows of his tour to promoters all over the country. He expected many of the dates to go into percentage, which meant he would make even more money than the guaranteed show contract. This is the way a tour like this works: If there are ten acts on a bus and each act costs $1,000 a week and plays 6 shows a week, adding in all other costs, the producer's total cost might be $2,000 per night. The producer (Tim, in this case) might sell the show for $3,500 per night to other promoters or theatres in other cities. The deal would be $3,500 per night or 60% of the gross sales, whichever was greater. If the show sold $10,000 worth of tickets, the promoter had to pay the producer $6,000 instead of the $3,500 guarantee. The producer would then make $4,000 instead of $1,500 on that one date.

Continuing his story Tim said, "Anyway, Patrick, to make a long story short, Dick Clark has offered me a job. It's a chance to head his department for great money and I can't turn it down. This man is gold. He is a powerhouse. Going up against him with Pitney was one of the best moves I ever made. Now here is where you come in. I told Dick that I could deliver Pittsburgh. What I want you to do is to take over my business. You promote all the concerts in the city but you'll be Dick Clark's partner on the concerts he offers you. You can still promote your own shows in Pittsburgh or anywhere else, but if Dick Clark wants to do one of his shows at the Civic Arena, you'll be obligated to do it with him. I'm talking Pittsburgh only. Anything you do outside the city is 100% yours, unless you want us in as a partner. You can take over my office here in suite 211. I've just signed an exclusive promoter's agreement with Charlie Strong for concerts at the Civic Arena. This gives you an exclusive on concerts at the Arena."

As if that wasn't enough, Tim had even more good news for me. "I also need you to take over a deal I just structured with AC Freeland at Conneaut Lake Park (an amusement park 94 miles north of Pittsburgh). I guaranteed him I would do a weekly show and dance at Dreamland Ballroom inside the park every Saturday night and on holidays and that I would also promote at least two concerts in their Convention Hall each summer. I did one there while you were in the Army last year and it sold out. The Convention Hall holds up to 4,500 people."

Finally he paused, took a long drag on his cigarette, and set it upright on its filter perpendicular to the ash tray, as he always did. I watched the smoke curl around his closed eye as he said, "I know I'm throwing a lot at you at one time, but this Dick Clark deal came up so fast. He won't let me have any side deals going. I have to get out from under of all these other deals, so I thought I'd throw them your way. What do you think?"

My head was spinning. "When will this all take place? When do you start with Dick?"

"Well, I still have to do my Gene Pitney tour to prove myself before we finalize the deal, but that won't be a problem. My show is strong and I think I can sell out on every date. He will realize that early on in the tour. He has two other tours going out at the same time but I think my show is better than either one of his and will have an overall higher gross. I think we'll have a deal before The Gene Pitney Shower of Stars is over in June. He needs someone to run his touring department now and I can do it. He has no one else. You should plan on taking over this office on June 1. You'll get everything that goes with it except Tammy. She has another job lined up."

"But Tim, where will I get the money I need to do this?"

"Look, this is a great opportunity for you. I'm not charging you anything for giving you my business. All you have to do is guarantee the Civic Arena that you will promote at least 10 concerts a year. The rent is $3,500 per date. You have to produce ten shows or pay the guarantee of $3,500 for each date you don't play. You also have 15 weeks' worth of shows to produce at Conneaut Lake at a cost of $300 per week to rent for the ballroom. You can handle that."

"But, Tim, I don't have any money."

"Pat, I'm going to tell you something I don't ever want you to forget. If you have to have all the money you need to do something before you do it, you will never do anything. I don't always have the money myself, but I don't let that stop me. I just do it and people buy tickets. It's simple psychology. You make people believe you have all the money you need even if you don't. People think we're big deals because we work with big name entertainers. You will never have all the money you need when you need it. Just make people believe you have whatever you need. They'll believe you and they'll help you."

I believed him.

Conneaut Lake Park

A few days later, Tim and I drove to Conneaut Lake Park. Tim wanted to honor the agreement he'd made with AC Freeland, the CEO, to promote dances each week and bring in two big summer concerts. I knew I had to act fast, as we were only two months away from Memorial Day and Tim had nothing booked yet. I had never been to the park, but I knew the area well because I had promoted records at many area radio stations within an hour's drive. I had never promoted a dance before, but I was confident I could do it. Compared to a full concert, a dance would be easy.

Mr. Freeland was a nice gentleman who made it clear that he didn't want any "wild music" in the park. He had a respectable property that had been in the family for decades and he wanted events that would enhance the family image of his park.

Tim assured him that I would do a great job and honor his

wishes. Mr. Freeland was agreeable. He thought that by bringing in younger acts, the park would attract a new audience, increase awareness, and bring in customers from as far as Pittsburgh, Buffalo, and Cleveland.

When we left the meeting I had a contract in hand to produce all Conneaut Lake Park's 1965 season concerts and dances. I still had no money, but AC Freeland didn't know that. I just followed Tim's advice and the psychology worked.

The park would be open from Memorial Day to Labor Day and I was to present a hit recording artist every weekend at its big weekly dance. As usual, I was starting out with a thousand questions and no answers. *Where would I get the money to pay for it all? Could I get any acts to go to Conneaut Lake, Pennsylvania? Could I deliver everything I had promised?*

My Beatles money from the previous September was gone. In truth, I did have a little money left from the $5,000 that Sonny and I each made from the Roundball Classic, but it was going quickly. I was spending it in the studio to record the groups I was managing and I bought a car. I had office and living expenses. I was no longer getting a paycheck. I wasn't broke, but I certainly didn't have what I needed to promote the Conneaut Lake Park shows…yet.

Conneaut Lake Park - First Dance

For the first dance at Conneaut Lake I booked a band called Question Mark and the Mysterians (which they spelled with a "?"), who had a current hit record called "96 Tears." I selected WGRP in nearby Greenville to promote the show and dance. I bought radio spots in Erie and Meadville, PA., and in nearby Youngstown, OH. I also bought ads in the local newspapers. Additionally, I distributed 300 posters to display on telephone poles and store windows in high traffic locations

Posters were always problematic. It's not easy to find dependable workers to put up 300 posters. They might put up a few where they knew I would see them and throw the rest in the trash, and I didn't have time to drive around to check on them all. But I did find one honest guy named Charlie Robbins. Charlie would come into all the record distributors in Pittsburgh to pick up records for the mom and pop record shops in the Beaver Falls, PA area. Charlie was in his sixties when I first met him at Regal Records. He was an adorable, unmarried, Jewish gentleman who lived at the YMCA in Beaver Falls and he knew everyone in Beaver County. He spent most of his life working in the circus and one of his many jobs was distributing hundreds of posters in each town where the circus played.

He would boast "We could never afford paper and radio advertising so we had to use posters. It was the cheapest and most effective way to advertise. I put them out there and people came to the show."

But Charlie didn't drive. He took the bus everywhere he went, and that's how he delivered his posters. "Buses go to the areas where there are the most people," he explained. "Each day I take a bus in a different direction and I walk a lot, too." He loved distributing posters for my Conneaut events.

"You are going to need help every Saturday at Conneaut. I don't live too far from there, could you pick me up? I can do the posters, work the show, and take tickets for you," he practically begged.

I loved the old guy and because I was in my twenties, he was rather fatherly toward me. He always had good advice to give and good circus promotion stories. I liked having him around. I was building a team and I valued his contribution.

Getting through the week was always stressful. *How could I have been so stupid?* I would think. *Where am I going to get the money to keep going?* And more and more, as I thought of these things, I was reaching for the vodka. At first, I mixed it with orange juice, but after a while, I just pulled a bottle out of desk drawer and drank it straight.

I had a few low dollar band bookings in the works—proms and local clubs—but those were 10% commission jobs and the bands only got $100 to $200 a night. I learned from Pete Tambellini how to put complete prom packages together for high schools and make up to 50% of the gross. It was a good deal for me and for the schools. On some of these dates, I could make $1,000 a night and still give the school a great show at a great price.

On the morning of that first Question Mark (?) and the Mysterians show my dad, brother Mike, Sonny Vaccaro, and I left Trafford for the drive to Beaver Falls to pick up Charlie, and then on to Conneaut Lake. "As soon as we get there," Charlie told us, "I'll put up more posters all around the area like I always did with the circus on the day of the show." Mike agreed to drive him around after dropping us off at the venue, where I met with AC Freeland and the head of security. The security guy was a real hick who talked down to me like I had never promoted a public event before.

"Well, you can never be too careful here," he told me. "Those city kids from Pittsburgh could tear this place to pieces. I told Mr. Freeland not to do these shows. They're going to be trouble, big time trouble. I called the Crawford County Police and the State Police, too, and asked them to be on the alert and ready for a riot."

"You want the State Police to sit around Conneaut Lake waiting for problems to happen that will probably never happen?" I asked him. "Do you really think we need that?"

"Why not? I'll have the state boys park their cars at the entrance as a show of force. The county guys will be inside the ballroom to back me up just in case there's a war."

"A war!? This isn't Vietnam, man! This is Conneaut Lake Park. There's no war here." I was getting concerned about this guy. I had been on active duty just a few months ago and I'd met enough trigger happy lunatics for one lifetime. Now this guy.

"Well, let me tell you something," he went on. "I've been doing this for a long time and I think I know what I'm doing.

You don't know about this place. Me? I live with it every day. If anything goes wrong here, I'll take the responsibility while you'll just take your money and go back to Pittsburgh. I have my reputation to watch out for," he boasted.

I couldn't believe this guy. But, I went along with him. I didn't think there would be any trouble—Conneaut Lake was a family place. This guy was dangerous. I could picture him with guns blazing if anything should happen. But he was part of the package, so I had to deal with him.

The band arrived in the late afternoon, two hours late. Dreamland Ballroom was on the second floor of a big building right in the middle of the park. The first floor housed a collection of small specialty shops selling souvenirs, ice cream, and knick-knacks. Across the walkway was a miniature golf course. The ten-foot wide steps leading up to the ballroom passed close to a "High Striker," a carnival game featuring a large bell, which patrons try to ring with a wooden hammer.

After the sound check the band went off to their hotel in the park to rest until show time. We should have gotten rooms ourselves, even though we weren't planning to stay overnight, just to rest during the down time. It would take us more than three hours to drive Charlie back to Beaver Falls and then go on home to Trafford. But we had no rooms so we just hung out, walking around the park until the anticipated start time of 8:00. We ran into the park manager, who reminded me that the dance must end by 11:30. We planned to play records until 9:30, bring on the band for its 45-minute show, then resume playing records until 11:30. I asked the DJ to play The Spaniels hit version of "Good Night Sweetheart" as the last song to let the audience know that the dance was over.

The DJ was a local guy who had been giving free plugs for the dance on his radio show. Radio DJ's could be the biggest hams. They had a tendency to take credit on the air for bringing the shows to town. I never wanted the credit myself. If the DJ wanted to make himself out to be a big deal, that was fine with me. All the equipment for the DJ was set up by the park. "I don't want anyone touching my equipment but me," said the park electrician. That, too, was fine with me because if the sound went off mid-show or didn't work correctly, the park couldn't blame me for it, and it saved me from having to truck in my own sound system at my own expense.

Charlie and Mike came back after 5:00 p.m. Since the sound check was over and the dance wasn't going to start until 8:00, we had a lot of time to kill so we decided to walk through the park towards the lake. The park was old but it was well kept, pleasant, and beautiful. Family cottages and boats lined the lakeshore and private cottages dotted the park throughout. It felt quite serene.

We dropped by the park cafeteria, which was built on stilts and jutted out over the lake, at about 5:00 p.m. Large, open windows provided patrons with a fine view of the peaceful lake. Leading us to our table, the hostess boasted that the view was even more beautiful at night, when all the boats were lit up and cruising around the lake. I would like to have seen that, but we would be working.

"Are you up here for the weekend?" she asked. "Do you have a boat?"

"No, we've never been here before. We are with the Dance and Show at Dreamland Ballroom."

Suddenly, she turned hostile. "Oh, so you're the ones putting on the show! I hope you don't cause a riot here! This is a nice place and we don't need any trouble! I wish you would just get out of here and take your rock and roll concerts back to Pittsburgh."

Obviously, we wouldn't be selling *her* any tickets to our shows!

Despite the objections of our hostess, I opened my briefcase and pulled out my folder for the night's event, which included a breakdown of costs: $300 for rental of the hall, $35 for the DJ, $120 for Crawford County Deputy security, $200 for advertising, $70 to print and distribute posters, $750 for the stars of the show, $150 for the opening act, etc. Total expenses: $1,825. With a $1.50 ticket price I had to sell 1,250 tickets just to break even. I was already broke. If I were to lose money on this show I could not have covered my costs. I had a crazy cop to deal with, negative attitudes from the locals, an uncertain market, and at that moment, Conneaut Lake Park was looking like a bad idea.

"Calm down, everything's going to be fine," Charlie reassured me. "I have a good feeling about tonight,"

We left the cafeteria at 6:40 for the long walk across the park to Dreamland Ballroom.

"I wonder why all those people are standing around the High Striker up ahead?" Mike asked. "There couldn't be that many people waiting in line just to hit a stupid ball with a hammer."

Just then, I saw Dick the park manager, along with A.C. Freeland's teenage sons, running toward us. *Oh, no. What now?* I thought.

Dick was agitated. "Where the heck have you been? We've been looking all over the park for you. The whole park is jammed up with kids waiting to get into your dance. You've got to get up there and open the box office. You've got to get the dance started now!"

Pushing our way through a crowd of teenagers toward the box-office, I shouted to the others, "Let's get this party started!"

That enormous crowd of kids was the most beautiful sight I had ever seen! AC Freeland himself said, "I've never seen anything like this."

It was exhilarating. "Tell the jock to start playing records," I told Mike. "Then get back here and help us sell tickets."

A few minutes later, he was back. "The DJ is playing records now," he informed me. It was not yet 7:00—an hour before the show was supposed to start—and it was already clear we had a successful show on our hands. We opened the doors and started selling tickets so fast we couldn't stop to stack the money. Charlie was stuffing torn tickets in his sport jacket pockets. Dad was dropping them in a cardboard box that was soon overflowing. There was money scattered on the box-office floor. We couldn't keep up. But who cared?

"Look at all that money," Dad said as he came into the box-office, "It's everywhere. We've got to get organized here."

"Yes, Dad, but it's a good problem to have, huh?" I joked. We had a full house!

The bands played on time, the crowd was peaceful, and the kids loved it. So did their parents. At the end of the dance, some of the parents came to the ticket booth and thanked us.

By midnight, with the dance over, I had paid everyone in cash and we had packed up to leave. AC Freeland was still there. The park cop who thought this was going to be Vietnam was with him. AC shook my hand and said, "Nice job, I hope they all go this well. Not a single problem. The crowd was well behaved. Let's talk on Monday and go over a few suggestions. Can you call me?"

"Thank you, sir. Yes, I will call you on Monday. Good night, Mr. Freeland. Good night, Chief." I said as I nodded and gave the cop a military salute.

It was a long drive home, but I was thrilled. Dad handed me a cigar box when we arrived back in Trafford with the final proceeds from the night—$4,500, after expenses. I was in business—$4,500 in one night. Conneaut Lake Park may have seemed like a bad idea early last evening after hearing that hostess complain, but it sure looked like a good idea now.

Not only did I have a whole summer's worth of dances to promote, I also had two big concerts at Conneaut Lake Convention Hall to plan. Dick Clark had two tours out that summer, one with Tom Jones and the other was The Four

Seasons featuring Frankie Valli. I played them at Convention Hall and they both sold out. It was the best summer of my life. By Labor Day, I had accumulated a $50,000 bankroll.

I would not have to worry about paying for my shows again for quite some time.

Chapter Eleven
The Syria Mosque and Beyond

Jethro Tull: September 11-12, 1973

In the spring of 1973 I received a call from Barbara Skydel, the vice president of Premier Talent Agency in New York and also one of its top agents. Premier represented many top acts and I booked all of them. The agency's president and CEO, Frank Barsalona, and I had a great relationship. Anytime he asked me for a favor, I delivered. In 1972, for instance, he was trying to sign a new act from the West Coast that looked promising, so he called me. "Pat, I'm working with a group from the coast called The Eagles. Could you help me get the record played? It's called "Take It Easy."

I was able to get the top stations in Pittsburgh to play the record even though they had not heard of the band. Of course, it was a great song that went on to become a smash hit and would have done so without my help, but hey, I was there for Frank when he needed me and he appreciated it.

Barbara Skydel was planning a U.S. tour for the British band, Jethro Tull. I had played Jethro Tull several times in different venues, starting in 1969 at the Electric Theatre and I always made money with them.

By 1973, I had earned a reputation as the top authority on the concert promotion business in Pittsburgh. I had the most important venues locked up—the Syria Mosque, a beautiful 3700 seat concert theatre, the 17,000 seat Civic Arena, and Three Rivers Stadium which could accommodate up to 60,000 concert fans. If an act wanted to perform in Pittsburgh, they had to go through me. This prompted Ed Masley of the *Pittsburgh Post-Gazette* to write, "If you expected to play Pittsburgh in the late '60s, pal, you either talked to Pat DiCesare or you stayed home."

Having Barbara Skydel call me, was a big deal at the time. Usually, I dealt with Richard Nader, who had once lived in nearby Masontown, Pennsylvania but moved to New York to become an agent. He later left Premier and went on to produce and promote the very successful "Rock and Roll Revival" series in Madison Square Garden and other major cities across the country.

For Barbara to call me directly it had to be something big. What she wanted was my availabilities for Three Rivers Stadium that summer."

I replied, "Okay, Barbara who's the act?"

"Never mind who the act is, just go and get me your availabilities," she demanded rather arrogantly. Barbara was always difficult to get on the phone and when you did get to talk with her you didn't do much talking yourself. She did.

I complied with her request. Hey, this was a ballpark date she was asking for—the ultimate concert event. Ballpark shows were always stressful. Anything could go wrong and usually did.

I called Three Rivers Stadium management and talked to Walter Golby, the general manager. "Walter, I need your availabilities for a rock concert. What dates do you have between Pirate games?" I asked.

"Who's the act?"

"I don't know yet but I need your open dates. I will need the stadium two days before the concert to set up before the show and one day to tear down after the show. Please give me any four consecutive days that you have open."

With a possible date in hand, I called Barbara back to relay the information. "Now can you tell me the name of the act?" I was excited about getting another ballpark show. If I made the right deal, it could mean a $50,000 night for me.

"Okay," she said, "I guess I can tell you now. It's Jethro Tull."

"How many other acts will they have on the show?"

"None. Just Jethro Tull."

I had to think about that for a minute. I couldn't believe that she thought Jethro Tull could sell 60,000 tickets.

"Don't you think Jethro Tull can sell out Three Rivers?" she asked.

"Absolutely not! I just played them last year and I don't think their product is that hot. Not hot enough for a ballpark date with no support acts."

"Well, hold the dates anyway," she again demanded.

The next day she called and informed me she had changed her mind and that Three Rivers Stadium might not be a good idea after all. She asked me to get the availabilities for two consecutive dates at the Civic Arena instead.

"You want me to do two dates at the arena?"

"Yes. You have a problem with that?"

"Jethro Tull can't sell out two dates at the Arena," I explained, "no way."

"Just get a lease for two dates and put them on sale. You'll sell them out."

"I'll do it if you insist, Barbara, but I don't think it's a good idea. Why don't we put just one show on sale and if it sells out we'll add a second night? "

"No. Put them both on sale at the same time."

"You're the boss, Barbara, but I think you're making a big mistake. If I put both shows on sale at the same time, I'll tell you what I think will happen. We will sell two half-houses. I think Jethro Tull may have difficulty selling out even one show. That's 17,000 tickets, Barbara. We'll be lucky to sell 8,500 tickets each night. Nobody is going to buy seats all the way in the back on the third level for the first night when they could buy seats down front on the second night. Let's just do one night and sell it out and bring them back next year." I pleaded, but to no avail.

Barbara was the ultimate egotist. She thought she was a genius. I thought to myself, *has she ever promoted a show herself? I know more about Pittsburgh than she does, why doesn't she listen to me?* But, that's the way it is with some agents—you had to play up to their egos or risk offending them and see them book their acts with a competitor in another city. So I reluctantly capitulated. "Whatever you want Barbara, I'll get the arena availabilities."

I booked the two dates, put both shows on sale, and it went just way I predicted. Both nights sold only half-houses.

On the night of the first date, I was in my usual spot during the opening act—the main box office. I was always in the box office settling the date for the tour manager and his accountant. Promoters very seldom get to watch the show. There are always too many fires to put out before and during a concert.

During the intermission, while I was still doing the accounting work, I received a call in the box office that Ian Anderson wanted to see me in his dressing room. I wondered what he wanted. Usually the artist is too nervous about going on stage to talk to anyone before the show begins. If there is going to be any interviews or people to meet, it would usually be after the performance.

The box office was located at the front entrance of the arena at gate two. The backstage area was all the way around the arena to the back. It was a long walk and I was worried. "What is the problem? Why does he want to see me?"

When I got to the star's dressing room, I knocked on the door. Ian himself opened the door, "Pat, nice to see you, come in and have a seat. Want something to drink?" He asked rather politely. After we finished some small talk, he said in his accent, "So tell me, Pat, what went wrong? I looked out at the audience and it is only half full. Why did you do two dates?"

I couldn't wait to tell him the truth. I told him about Barbara insisting on the two dates and I only wanted one. I told him about the Three Rivers Stadium idea and expressed my opinion that she didn't know what she was doing. I told him the truth. After all, why should *I* look stupid? He let me go on ranting and raving about Barbara. While I was talking to him I suddenly realized that I was making a big mistake! I was yet to realize just how costly of a mistake that I was making, but it felt good telling someone that I was right and Barbara was wrong. When I was done, explaining what a genius I was and how Barbara didn't know what she was doing, he picked up the phone which was on an end table right beside the sofa where he was seated with his legs crossed and immediately called Barbara at her home and told her verbatim, of our conversation. He was on the phone for what seemed an eternity not only for me, but Barbara, I'm sure. He kept asking her why she wanted to do the two dates when I insisted on doing only one.

When Ian had finished his conversation and hung the phone up, he said, "Barbara would like you to call her tomorrow."

"Okay, is there anything else?"

"No, I better get ready to start the show. I go on in a few minutes."

The next morning I didn't have to call Barbara, she called me the very first thing. "How could you tell Ian that it was my idea? How stupid are you? Don't you ever, ever think you are getting another show from Premier! I will go to any other city but Pittsburgh with all of my acts!" She screamed. She wouldn't talk to me again. To this day I have never spoken to her. I never got another one of Premier's acts for some time. She helped establish a competitor in Pittsburgh and went out of her way to encourage outside promoters to go after me with a vengeance.

Fortunately for me, Barry Bell, who was a good friend of mine and an agent at the William Morris Agency was leaving William Morris and going over to Premier Talent. He had a good relationship with Bruce Springsteen and was bringing Bruce with him to Premier and would be the responsible agent for Bruce. Barry was assigned to be my agent for Premier. If I didn't get that lucky break, I would not have been able to book any of Premier's acts—not if Barbara had anything to say.

I learned a lot about life doing those two Jethro Tull dates. I was getting too sure of myself and forgot what it was like when I first started. Even though I was climbing the ladder of success quickly, I still needed people who could help me. I wasn't going to get those people or that help if I acted like a 'know it all' even if I thought I was right. I learned the lesson again that my mother had taught me a long time ago, "When you know you are right bite your tongue and say nothing."

Almost 40 years later, Brian Drusky, a former DiCesare-Engler employee, promoted Jethro Tull in concert at the Carnegie Library Theatre in the nearby steel mill town of Homestead, just a few miles from the Civic Arena and the stadium. Brian invited me to be his guest at the capacity crowd 1,100 seat theatre. When I arrived, Brian took me backstage to meet and say hello to Ian. We talked briefly and his wife took a picture of us. Ian did not remind me of the half-sold Civic Arena dates so long ago and I wasn't about to remind him, either.

Barbara Skydel, a legend in the rock and roll agency business, died of cancer in 2010.

The Syria Mosque

The "Mosque" as we most often referred to it, was the granddaddy of all the concert halls in Pittsburgh. Dedicated on October 26, 1916, it was built primarily to house the activities of the Syria Temple. Its members, who engaged in charitable work and fundraising, were called Shriners. Ten years later, The Pittsburgh Symphony began performing there on a regular basis. All the great artists performed at the Mosque, including Jascha Heifetz, Arthur Rubinstein, and Van Cliburn, along with great guest conductors like Leopold Stokowski, Arturo Toscanini and Eugene Ormandy. The Pittsburgh Opera also performed there from 1963 to 1971 until they moved (along with The Pittsburgh Symphony) to beautiful new Heinz Hall. All the jazz greats like Duke Ellington, Louis Armstrong, Billy Eckstine, Errol Garner, Count Basie, Benny Goodman, Art Tatum, Sarah Vaughn, and Dizzy Gillespie also performed at the Mosque during the thirties and forties.

In the early 70s, as the more highbrow shows moved to the more modern Heinz Hall, The Mosque became *the* place for rhythm and blues and rock and roll shows. Mosque management was not particularly keen on replacing the symphony, the opera, and great jazz concerts with the new rowdiness of rock. They remembered the Mosque's first rock shows during the 50s with Bill Haley and the Comets, James Brown, Chuck Berry, and Jerry Lee Lewis, when the audiences would jump up and down on the cushioned seats and damage their once quiet facility.

As revenues from concert dates began to dwindle in the mid-60s, the Mosque started taking a more aggressive and pragmatic approach and they allowed Tim Tormey and me to promote rock concerts there on a regular basis. Management appreciated our careful selection of artists and offered us an exclusive lease for rock shows. Our guarantee was that we would only bring acts with more sedate followings who were not likely to get too wild and cause damage. Nevertheless, if it had been up to Miss Steele, the manager of The Mosque, the theater would have hosted only the Symphony, the Opera or the Ballet, or otherwise be closed. But, she didn't have that power. The board needed revenue and the only way to do that was to work with promoters who would bring in top rock, pop, and R&B artists, who could easily sell out its 3,700 seats.

Unfortunately, Miss Steele, an older, unmarried, robust woman with a huge bosom and a derriere to match, didn't understand that music had changed over the past decades and would never be the same. She just didn't like rock music. I had to guarantee her there would be no smoking (back when smoking was permissible in public buildings), no profanity, no drugs, no loud music, that the patrons must remain seated during the performance at all times, and that the aisles be kept clear. Her demands were impossible for me to guarantee, but I assured her I could guarantee that and there would be no problems.

I was sincere in my attempt to please her, and I hoped the loud music would keep her in her office during the show, but that was never the case. She insisted, whenever I had a concert, on standing in the wings at stage right, where she had a good view of the artist and of the audience. She insisted I stay there next to her in case things got out of order.

Bette Midler 1973

One artist who I thought would sell tickets, be a crowd pleaser, and also be acceptable to Miss Steele was Bette Midler. It was 1973 and Bette was a newer artist with a big hit remake of "Boogie Woogie Bugle Boy" from her successful LP *The Divine Miss M. Miss Steele **has** to like her,* I thought. I could feel the excitement as soon as we put the tickets on sale. They sold quickly. On the day of the show, we did her sound check during the afternoon and after Bette did her bit, I thought to myself, "This is going to be a peaceful night." I watched the rehearsal, sitting down front and in the center, and approached Bette when it was over to tell her how happy I was she was playing the Mosque and that the sellout crowd would surely love her. She was happy to hear it was a sellout. That's all that any artist wants to hear. Most stars are insecure and sellouts feed their egos.

As I left the auditorium and started walking towards Miss Steele's office to tell her how great Bette was and that tonight shouldn't be a problem, I heard a voice from behind me shouting my name, "Mr. DiCesare! Mr. DiCesare!" I stopped and turned around and there was this skinny looking kid with a face that reminded me of a squirrel walking towards me.

"Thanks, for stopping Mr. DiCesare. I just wanted to talk to you for a moment. You are the promoter for the concert this evening?"

"Yes. Yes I am," I replied, wondering *who is this person and what does he want? Probably Bette's autograph.*

"I just wanted to introduce myself. I'm Miss Midler's musical conductor. My name is Barry Manilow and some day, Mr. DiCesare, you will be promoting *me* in concert. Some day I am going to be the star and the headliner."

Yeah kid, sure, I thought to myself. *Fat chance someone like you could be a star in this business. Don't quit your day job.*

Barry Manilow went on to write 'Friends' for Bette on her *The Devine Miss M* LP, and then record mega hits like "Mandy", "Looks Like We Made It," "Copacabana," and too many others to mention. Just as he promised, he became a star and I did promote him as the headliner. It just goes to show you how much I know.

It was a great night for the audience, who loved Bette, and a great night for Bette. But they loved her so much they did exactly what I didn't want them to do. They stood on their seats, smoked, danced in the aisles, and Bette cussed on stage like a sailor. Miss Steele's huge bosom shook like Jello as she shook her finger and yelled at me in her high pitched voice, "You lied to me! You told me this would be a quiet evening. I'll never believe you again. You won't ever promote another show in here again. You told me that I could trust you. Do you hear her swearing up there? Look at that audience out there in the aisles dancing and standing on the seats. Do you see them? Do something. Or I'll do something."

She was yelling so loud at me that Bette could hear her on stage and looked over to see what was causing this outburst.

I have to calm this woman down, I said, "Yes, Miss Steele, what would you like me to do?"

"What would I like you to do? You better think of something young man or I'm stopping this show right now!" While she was screaming at me she walked towards Bette, who was at the microphone singing, glancing warily at her, obviously wondering what the hell was going on offstage.

When Bette ended the song she looked at Miss Steele and me at stage right and saw Miss Steele shaking a finger at her. Miss Steele was demanding that I walk up to Bette on stage and scold her for not acting like a lady. I tried to reason with Miss Steele. "The show is almost over," I pleaded. "Just let her finish."

"No!" she insisted. She demanded that I confront Bette on stage—which was about the worst thing I could have done— tell her to quit swearing, and tell the audience to sit down in their seats, quit smoking, and behave themselves, or the show would not go on.

I felt stupid, but I had no choice. So I attempted to deliver Miss Steele's demands. Bette had the audience right where she wanted them. And for me to walk up to her in the middle of her performance and slow the momentum was absurd. As I approached Bette at her mic she looked at me angrily and said "What the fuck are you doing?"

"Bette, I'm sorry but the building manager is coming down on me and wants to stop the show until everyone sits down." I could tell the crowd was confused and some started shouting for the show to continue.

"I'm not telling them to sit down. What is this, grade school? If she doesn't knock it off, I'm walking off this stage and then you'll have *real* trouble."

The crowd started chanting, "Get off the fucking stage." It was the Janis Joplin show all over again.

"Where is the person who told you to talk to me?" Bette asked. I reluctantly pointed to Miss Steele, standing in the wings.

"Yeah, I thought that was her. Okay, I see her. Everything will be fine. I'll take care of it. You can leave now. Don't worry."

I walked from her microphone stand towards Miss Steele feeling relieved. There was a second of silence. The audience could sense what was happening and was anticipating Bette's message. Miss Steele, who looked much taller than her six-foot-plus frame, had her arms crossed above her mammoth, unattractive bust, and her lips were pursed. Bette grabbed the microphone with her one hand and pointed toward Miss Steele with the other and yelled, "That fucking bitch with the big tits wants me to quit swearing and wants you to sit down. You know what I say? Fuck her! Now I want everyone to stand up on your seats! We're going to rock this house all night long."

Miss Steele was so humiliated she turned and walked away in the direction of her office while yelling at me, "You're going to pay for this, DiCesare! You think you pulled something over on me! We'll see about that young man!"

I had tried to warn her numerous times that her management techniques just didn't work in today's world. You can't discipline a star when she's onstage performing. She couldn't understand this not the Opera.

After Bette's performance I had the unpleasant task of going to Miss Steele's office to settle the business of the show. I dreaded going into her office. I knew I was in trouble. My very future depended on appeasing both the star and Miss Steele. I couldn't have Bette telling her agent in New York that I was a lousy promoter. At the same time I couldn't have Miss Steele stop me from doing my shows. And at the moment, I had people to pay in her office so I didn't want her creating a scene.

To survive in the promotions business you need a good reputation. You have to pay your people on time—immediately after the performance. Some promoters had bad reputations for *not* paying on time, or at all, and that is why theaters and agents make promoters put up large deposits or pay in advance. I was fortunate! I had earned a reputation for paying everyone after the show without fail.

With my reputation, I didn't have to pay the radio stations until the end of the month. I never put up a fifty percent deposit for the artist, as most promoters had to do. I paid after the performance. Most acts demanded that a fifty percent deposit be paid at the signing of the contract and the other half paid before they went onstage. I didn't have to do that.

But this was now a very uncomfortable situation for me. I quickly paid Bette's road manager in her dressing room and thanked Bette for doing a great job. I had to keep her away from Miss Steele. I hurried out of the star's dressing room before anybody said anything negative.

Walking into the theatre office, I saw Miss Steele slumped at her desk with both hands under her chin. Mr. Wieland, the general manager, was sitting at his desk, looking as though he was sleeping. He had been with the Mosque forever and was well into his eighties. Maybe he is sleeping, I thought he could be sleeping. Clearly, Miss Steele was upset and I feared she was about to take it all out on me.

There was a brief silence, neither of us saying a word, until she pushed the expense statement in front of me and pointed with her pencil to the line, "Amount Owed." Sternly she said, "You will never do another show in this building—ever. I will tell the board. They'll hear about this in the morning. No more shows for you!"

"But Miss Steele, I looked in the auditorium, I don't think there are any damaged seats." I didn't know if that was exactly true, but it was the only defense I had. I knew that wasn't the issue anyway. She wasn't even thinking of the damages. She was upset because Bette humiliated her from the stage.

"I don't care," she said. "You bring these filthy-mouthed people in here who don't know how to behave, and the language they use! You ought to be ashamed of yourself for having anything to do with people like that. I'll have the maintenance people check for damages. You'll have to pay and there will be no more shows!"

Richard Pryor 1973

Later, I had to call Miss Steele for another date. I was hoping she might have cooled off by then.

"Hi, Miss Steele, I'm calling to see if you have an available date for a great show." I asked.

"Who?" she asked.

"Richard Pryor. He's a comedian." I answered.

"A comedian? Well maybe that will be alright. At least it's not one of these loud, profane rock and roll devil acts. That should be a quiet night." She had to add, "But no more of that filthy mouthed garbage, you understand?"

"No, Miss Steele. There will be no more of that filthy mouthed garbage and I guarantee you this will be a peaceful show"

There was no use disagreeing with her, but I knew there was nothing I could do about the behavior of an artist on stage. I kept hoping a miracle would happen and she would retire. God knows both she and Mr. Wieland were way past retirement age. She was still thinking like it's the 1920s when the symphony first started using the place. She was out of it and so was Mr. Wieland. The business had passed them by.

I kind of figured she didn't know anything about Richard and I didn't tell Miss Steele that Richard Pryor was a black comedian. Since the day James Brown performed there in the early 50s and drove his audience wild, she had been wary of black artists, especially black artists who appealed to a younger audience.

On the night of the show, Richard didn't show up until the intermission was almost over and it was time to go on. My agent friend, Bob Astor, once taught me about getting acts to arrive on time. Bob was a former musician from Metairie, Louisiana who traveled with the big bands when he was younger. He quit the road and now was a great New York agent. He asked me for the "time of performance" I wanted written on the contracts with the artist, I said, "Bob, I usually start all of my concerts at 8:00 p.m."

"Okay. 7:00 p.m."

"No, Bob. I said 8:00 p.m."

"Yeah, I know you want to start the show at 8:00 but I have to use 7:00."

"Why?"

"It's something I got from the old R&B bands in the 50s. They told me, 'If you want an act to show up at 8:00, you have to tell us 7:00. Then you stand a good chance we'll make it on time. But, don't hold your breath.'"

I made sure the show started on time and the opening act for Richard would be well behaved, according to Miss Steele. When intermission was over she walked toward the stage and I followed her like a school boy. The DJ from the radio station who was emceeing the show announced Richard Pryor. Miss Steele took her usual position in the wings on stage right, standing as close to me as possible. As the crowd applauded, Richard walked on to the stage, grabbed the microphone, and said, "How are you honkies doing?" The audience response wasn't what Richard wanted so he repeated his question a little louder, but added a few words.

"Okay! Let's try it again. How are you *motherfucking* honkies doing?" he shouted. Just as he expected, the mostly white crowd loved it and they started to cheer him on.

Miss Steele gasped and yelled, "You see! Do you hear what he's saying? You lied to me again. That's it for you. You go up there right now and tell him to stop it right now. We don't want swearing in this building."

"Miss Steele, I can't do that. It's called freedom of speech. He has rights. Do you think I like to hear this?"

"No swearing." she screamed. "Not in this building. Don't you ever bring him back! And as for you, Pat DiCesare, this is your last show here." She left the stage area headed toward her office and stayed there for the remainder of his performance. But she could still hear every word he said as he continued his string of profanities.

Later, when the show was over and the crowd having peacefully exited, I paid Richard. I didn't say a word to him about Miss Steele. Why spoil a good relationship? I did spend a few minutes in his dressing room reminiscing about Tim Tormey's Zanzibar Night Club in Pittsburgh, before Richard hit it big, when he came in asking for a job. It was a black night club and Tim had a lot of big stars performing there. Richard wanted to perform on stage. Tim told Richard he couldn't book him because no one knew him, but he did need a dishwasher, to which Richard responded, "Yeah, I know. That's why I came in. I want the dishwasher's job, but someday I'm going to be on your stage. I'm a comedian."

Richard Pryor took the job as the dishwasher. One night he came to work dressed in a suit and wearing a big smile. "Richard, aren't you too dressed up tonight to wash the dishes?" Tim asked him.

"I'm not washing the dishes tonight, Mr. Tim. Tonight I'm going to be on your stage."

"You are?"

"Yes, Mr. Arthur Prysock is letting me open his show tonight."

Tim said, "Okay, but you still have to wash the dishes."

I complimented Richard on his show and I left as quickly as I could. I never cared to hang out long in the dressing room with the acts. But I dreaded what I had to do next. I had to pay Miss Steele her expenses for the evening. I didn't look forward to that chore. I felt I was going to the principal's office for doing something wrong in school. But to my surprise, she appeared to have settled down and she calmly asked me "By the way, what is a honkie?"

"I don't know," I lied. I couldn't tell her that it was Richard's way of making fun of white people. The word "honkie" was for blacks what the N word was for whites. It was an insult. He spent the whole show hurling insults at his all-white audience and they ate it up.

171

This is the way it went for years between Miss Steele and me. Every show was my last, according to her, yet the board continued to retain me as Syria Mosques exclusive concert promoter. I promoted countless concerts there until we bought The Stanley Theatre in 1977. What a relief it was to finally own our own theatre. I never had to worry about getting chewed out by Miss Steele again, and I had no desire to promote another show at The Mosque again. Not until Jim Ecker called us almost seven years later...but that's another story.

Chapter Twelve
Summer Mini Tour, 1965

Throughout my early career I was constantly coming up with new, but untested and unproven ideas. I didn't always know if I had the time or the ability to bring these ideas to fruition, or if I could even afford to try. Yet I would jump into them without doing my due diligence, and sometimes that got me into trouble.

One of these ideas was a mini-Shower of Stars show. Instead of a concert, it would be a show and a dance. I got the idea during a discussion with Tim Tormey, Jack Hooke and Dick Clark one night at Al and Dick's Steakhouse in New York. We had finished our steaks and Tim and Jack were engaged in a deep discussion at the table when Dick asked me to join him at the bar, "I have a question for you, Pat," he said. "What do you think about taking the Caravan of Stars into the tertiary markets? People who live in small towns never get to see any shows in their own backyards and I think they just might come out in droves for a show like ours."

"I think it's too much of a risk, Dick," I responded honestly as I sipped my scotch and water. "These towns don't have enough people to fill 3,000 seats, and many of them couldn't or wouldn't pay big city prices. I just don't think it will do well."

"Oh well, it was just a thought," he said as we walked back towards the table, "Let's keep that between the two of us." Maybe he didn't want Tim or Jack to hear what might be a dumb idea. Later, I thought more about it and the idea prompted me to come up with a "Mini Show and Dance" promotion of my own for these small markets. If I could attract 1,000 to 3,000 local kids to a dance at only a buck or a buck-fifty and keep my costs low, I could make money. It would be similar to what I was doing at Conneaut Lake, but instead of promoting just one event a week in one location, I would promote an event every night in a different town. If I could score like I was scoring at Conneaut, it could be big.

The idea was to buy a headliner act for one week and put that act on the road with a strong support act, a backup band, and a DJ. I would rent seven dance halls in seven different towns seven nights a week and that would be my circuit. I would work the circuit with a different set of acts every week. I would start by approaching the top rock disc jockey in each town I was considering and make a deal for $35 to $50 a week (depending on how powerful his station was) for plugging the show and dance and playing my acts' records in heavy rotation the week of the dance. To sweeten the pot, I would buy a package of radio spots for around $100 each week from the sales manager. To these guys who owned radio stations in small towns, that was a sizable sale, and it would be a good deal for both of us.

The stations I approached agreed to announce the artist's names during the weather break and when announcing the time of the day and the news break. They would promote the show constantly because it was the only thing really happening in most of these towns. They asked me to bring in bigger concerts, as well, to play their small town version of the Civic Arena—a National Guard Armory, a high school gymnasium, or a small theatre. I promised to bring in concerts to their towns if the dances were successful, hoping that might motivate them to work the show even harder.

Tim always said, "There are three parts to the promotion business: first, you need a venue—a theatre, a gym, an arena. Second, you must tell everybody about the show and you keep telling them about it over and over, and just when you think that everyone knows, you tell them again. And third is the show itself. You must be able to accomplish these three tasks for less money than most wannabe's could ever even think about and if you can and if you do, then you can rightfully call yourself a promoter.

I could and I was.

I made great deals with all the venues and persuaded the building managers to provide some extra services at no charge. They viewed me as a good customer who was renting their facilities every week throughout the summer for my dances and bringing in even bigger shows once or twice a year, as well. They wanted me to be successful.

The radio stations and the DJ's felt the same way. I advertised primarily with radio spots and posters. I didn't pay the same rate for radio spots that the average Joe selling shoes or water heaters paid. Their rate cards didn't apply to me. I would get more like $500 worth of spots for $100 along with countless free mentions by the DJ's like, "Here's another song by Sam the Sham and The Pharaohs. Don't forget they will be at the big show and dance this week at the Nathan Goff Armory. You better get your tickets now at Broadway Records because they're going fast." They called that a "promo" and I didn't have to pay for it. That was better than a paid spot. The stations were willing to do that because they were proud to be presenting my shows in their towns, where few promoters had ever been before.

The ticket locations loved me and were willing to sell my tickets at no cost because they got on-air promotion from the radio spots and the DJ's and that would drive traffic to their stores. I pointed out to the owners the public perception was that the promoters selected the biggest and best store in town to sell their tickets.

Also, I was able to buy the acts cheaper because I was buying them for the week. At that time, the big agency for me was Premier Talent in New York, run by Frank Barsalona.

The two agents I dealt with most were Barbara Skydel and Richard Nader. Richard liked dealing with me because he was from Masontown, PA, close to Pittsburgh. He knew well of my reputation in Pittsburgh.

Normally, when any promoter called Premier Talent to buy an act like the Crystals, for example, who had several hits to their credit, Richard, the agent, would charge them perhaps $500 a night and the promoter would have to supply a local band to back up the girls. But when I called him to buy the Crystals for a week, he was more negotiable. "The Crystals get $2,500 for a week," he said, "but I will personally ask them to do it for you for $2,000. Of course, you'll need to pay their expenses on top of that." In the end I would typically end up getting a $500 a night act for only $300.

I did the same with the backup band. I would give the band copies of the groups' hits. They would rehearse the songs and play the instrumental back up for the headliner and other opening acts. Often, the songs were so simple and familiar to the band that I didn't even have to give them the records—they could play the songs by memory. The backup band, usually a band I was managing and recording myself, would play a few songs before we brought the opening act on and use their spot to play and promote their own records. I made sure they had a new release to promote and I introduced them to the local jocks, who were happy to play their records on the air as part of their promotion of the show. This helped me establish my bands in these towns for future bookings. The bands loved it and I always advertised them as "Bobby Records recording artists."

My deal with the acts and the backup band was that once they got to Pittsburgh for the beginning of the tour I would provide and pay for their transportation, meals, and hotels. I provided a car and a driver to take the act from town to town so I would have control over the act and be sure that they showed up on time every night. I would drive my own crew—my brother Mike, Sonny Vaccaro and Charlie Robbins—around to the shows myself.

Coordinating all of these shows in all these towns was a big job, and because we were playing seven nights a week for fifteen weeks, no one got a night off. I was on the road with these guys every day and at the same time I still had a business to run back at the office. It was intense and exhausting.

The First Week: Dickey Lee

For the first week of my small-town summer mini-tour I selected Dickey Lee as the headliner. Dicky's biggest hit was "Patches," a tragic waltz about a teenage couple from different economic backgrounds. The boy's father won't let him date her because she's from the wrong side of the tracks, so she drowns herself, and the boy follows suit the next night. The resulting controversy over the story line spurred the record on to become a million-seller. Dickey followed it with a couple of minor hits before scoring big again with yet another teen tragedy titled "Laurie." When I found out I could buy Dickey for a week for only $750 I was ecstatic. I didn't even try to beat the agent down on the price. I was getting a national multi-hit recording artist for only $100 a night! That was unbelievable! *I'll sell out every date,* I thought.

I figured it would be like Conneaut Lake Park. I'll make $3,000 a night—$21,000 for the week. I planned to promote 15 weeks of summer shows, which meant I could potentially earn around $300,000 that summer. Throwing in three or four concerts to the schedule would add another $100,000 to the bottom line. *I'll be rich*, I thought. *I'll dump my little studio apartment get a full-size apartment at the new Washington Plaza apartments they're building near the Civic Arena. I'll have an interior designer I know furnish the place. And I'll buy a Cadillac, too!* I was thinking big.

The tour schedule was as follows: Johnstown, PA on Monday; Fairmont, West Virginia on Tuesday; Clarksburg, West Virginia on Wednesday; Parkersburg, West Virginia on

Thursday; Geneva-on-the-Lake, Ohio on Friday; Conneaut Lake Park, PA on Saturday; and Tom Hartman's Red Rooster in Greensburg, PA. on Sunday.

Dickey Lee arrived at my office at The Carlton House on that first Monday afternoon. My brother Mike was at the wheel for the two-and-a-half hour drive to Johnstown, with Charlie Robbins in the front passenger seat, Sonny Vaccaro, Dickey and me in the back. We talked about the entertainment business the whole way there. I have to admit that for the first time in my life I was actually impressed being with a huge star like Dickey. He was such a down-to-earth guy, you had to like him. When we arrived in Johnstown I took Dickey directly to WCRO Radio for a live interview with Larry Crow. Larry always played any record I needed to be pushed. The station played a mix of adult, country, and rock. Its top jock was Herb Ruth, who had done a good job plugging the show and would be spinning the records for the dance that night.

The Johnstown venue was the local high school gym. It was summer and the kids were out of school and I was confident we would do well. I figured my expenses to be about $1,100. The admission price was $1.50 which I didn't think was too high, but Johnstown kids were accustomed to paying around 50 cents to go to a dance, especially at their high school gym. I needed 750 kids to break even for the night. My optimism was fueled by the enthusiasm of the DJ's from the radio station. I put my trust in their knowledge of the market.

Johnstown was a tough town for me when I promoted and sold records there before going into the army. The town seemed to always be in a recession. It was a typical Pennsylvania industrial town full of steel mills, railroads, and coal mines. At the retail level, business always seemed to be bad. Even so, after coming off the gigantic show and dance at Conneaut Lake Park just a few days earlier on the Memorial Day weekend, I thought we might see as many as two or three thousand kids show up and that I would easily hit my $20,000 per week goal.

Boy was I wrong! What I didn't realize was there was

already too much competition for the Johnstown teenagers' money—proms, graduation ceremonies, graduation parties, and weddings. To make it worse, Monday just wasn't a party night for these kids, not even to see a hit recording artist like Dicky Lee. We ended up with a paid attendance of only 400 kids—a miserable $600 in ticket sales. What made the loss even worse was having to play to such a dismal crowd for three-and-a-half hours. When Dicky took the stage, the sparse crowds pushed right up to the stage, making the cavernous facility seem emptier. It was embarrassing for both Dickey and me and I felt sorry for Dickey having to perform to such a small crowd.

It was a long drive back home that night. I had to drop off Mike and Sonny in Trafford and Charlie in Beaver Falls and I didn't get home until 3:00 in the morning. All this aggravation had just cost me $500. Dickey spent the night on a foldout cot in my office next door to my apartment.

I stayed up after saying goodnight to Dicky to review what had just happened. Where did I go wrong? What mistakes had I made and how could I prevent making them again? As I said at the start of this chapter, sometimes I jump into things without doing my due diligence and I concluded my first error in judgment was selecting Dickey Lee for the first show. I really liked the guy and he did have some huge hits, but he just wasn't a headliner. He would be great as one of the acts for a "Dick Clark Caravan of Stars" show or our own Pittsburgh version with "The Shower of Stars" when we put 13 acts on a bus and toured the country. The sheer size of such a show, with so many hit acts, was exciting enough to draw big crowds.

But Dickey alone was not enough. And his big hit wasn't an exciting dance song—it was a waltz! What was I thinking? Also, Dickey was a solo singer at a time when most hit acts were self-contained bands that played their own instruments and sang their own original songs. The Rolling Stones, The Beatles, the Beach Boys, even the Four Seasons—that's what kids wanted now. I knew from promoting records that groups who played music loud and fast out-old solo artists who sang soft, smooth ballads. Sure there will always be Sinatra and Mathis and other great ballad singers, but with the genre I was working in, the kids wanted their music loud and fast. They wanted great *bands*. No wonder no one showed up.

To make it worse, Monday was just not a good night for a dance, and Tuesdays weren't much better. Maybe four nights a week was enough. Sure, my cost per night for the headliner would increase, but why risk promoting on the worst nights of the week? Oh well, maybe tomorrow night won't be so bad, I hoped, trying to console myself, but it wasn't working. I was punishing myself for being so stupid. Opening my kitchen cabinet, I reached for the scotch and as I poured myself a tall one, vowing never to let this happen again. I fell asleep at my desk with the unfinished drink in my hand.

"I Feel at Home, Sergeant."

Tuesday nights' dance was to be held at The National Guard Armory in Fairmont, West Virginia. I had promoted a concert at the same armory years ago with Tim. I remembered it being a nice venue. Upon arriving that afternoon I went directly to the office of the Sergeant who was in charge of the facility. I knocked on his door and waited until hearing his command, "Enter." I was reminded of my months on active duty in the reserves, which I didn't particularly like.

"Hello, Sergeant," I began, "I'm Pat DiCesare and I'm with the show tonight,"

"Hi, Pat, I've been waiting for you. We're all set up for your event this evening," he said in a cheerful manner. He wasn't at all like most of the facility managers. He seemed calm. I guess being in the army he had seen a lot more action and stress than a dance could provide. It was a welcome relief. "So how do you feel?" he inquired.

"I feel at home, Sergeant," I said.

"What do you mean by that?"

"I was discharged just last November from Fort Sill. I see you are an artillery unit—105 Howitzers. That was my outfit, too. I still go to reserve meetings in Pittsburgh. So I feel at home in this armory." I explained.

"I was told that you were with Dick Clark, doing shows all over the country?"

"I am and I do when he has a show. Otherwise I do my own shows, like tonight's show and dance," I replied.

"How can you go to reserve meetings when you have to travel so much? Don't you go two weekdays and a weekend every month?"

"I sure do and yes, it is difficult for me to make the meetings."

"Would you like to get out of going to all those reserve meetings? What do you have, about 5 more years?"

"That's correct, Sarge, but what do you mean about not going to the meetings?" More than anything else in my life, I and most every other reservist I knew hated being in the reserves at this time. It was better than being drafted, but after doing our 6 months of active duty, we had 5 ½ more years in the reserves and we had to be ready to return to active duty at a moment's notice. That meant the possibility of going to Vietnam. None of us wanted that. Reserve meetings were a big waste of time. Two Tuesday evenings plus one weekend a month from 6:00 to 10:00 p.m. I had to drive 45 minutes from my home to the Hunt Armory in the Shadyside area of Pittsburgh and play soldier. Usually, we just stood around trying to look and act busy to pass the time away. We were bored and most of the time we stood around drinking coffee and smoking cigarettes. I didn't smoke myself and the smell of cigarettes made me sick, so that only made things worse.

One weekend a month we had to stay for 8 hours on Saturday and 8 hours on Sunday and every summer we had to go to a camp for two full weeks, in addition to the weeknight meetings. I didn't know how I could to do that with all the business I had going on and neither did most of the other guys in my unit. As I spoke to the sergeant I was painfully aware that my two weeks was coming up in just six weeks, in the middle of July, and right in the middle of my summer concert schedule.

The sergeant said to me, "Look, I want to show you something. Here's a pencil and some paper. I want you to write this down. Whatever you do, don't tell anyone I gave you this information."

He turned around and reached for a book that he kept in a shelf behind his desk and he flipped through several pages and said, "Here it is, right here," and he started to mutter to himself as he flipped through some notes. "Let's see, it's page, hmm, one sec, hmm, it states here that if you have a job that requires you to be out of the area and you are unable to attend these meetings, then you shall be excused. That means you don't have to attend the meetings, but you are still in the National Guard. If you are needed, they can call you back in at any time and you must go or you will be drafted and have to start all over. If you don't go, they will probably throw you in the stockade. So if you get called back in—go! All you need is a letter from Dick Clark's office explaining your situation as being vital to the business."

"Are you telling me that because I promote rock concerts the Army will classify me as being vital to someone's business and exempt me from attending meetings?" I asked. It was hard to believe I could get out of it that easily. That was too good to be true!

"Look," the Sergeant said, "the Army and National Guard have all kinds of stupid rules that don't have to make sense. If you want to get out of it legally, just do what I tell you and don't tell anyone I was the one who gave you this info. That would be a career killer for me."

"Well, thank you, Sergeant. I'll do it. I really do appreciate this and I won't tell anyone you told me."

"Good. Now let's talk about tonight. What do you need? Let's go look at the stage and the set up," he said.

I was too excited about what he just told me to even think

about the event that evening. I couldn't wait to call Tim's office to get a letter on Dick Clark's letterhead explaining how I was crucial to his business. *Who knows? It just might work!*

The Fairmont show did a little better than Johnstown. We had about 500 paid attendance. The sergeant kindly pleaded with me not to get discouraged. "This thing will build up and get better each week. You have to promise me you'll bring in more shows to our Armory."

Even though I had lost money, I didn't care. "Yes, I will come back," I assured him. If that's what it would take to get out of those tedious reserve meetings I would gladly do more shows at the Fairmont Armory.

The next morning I called Tim in New York with the news and asked the $64,000 question, "Will Dick give me the letter?"

"Pat, I will do everything to help you, you know that," he said.

Two days later, I received a copy in the mail of the letter Tim sent special delivery to the proper authorities in the Reserve and within a month I received letter from them excusing me from any further meetings unless there was a national emergency requiring me to rejoin the unit. They made it clear that I still had a 6-year obligation to the Reserve and if the war worsened I could be called to active duty within 24 hours. But for the moment, I was relieved from attending meetings. Of all the things in my life I owe to the music business, saving me from active duty in the Reserves, and possibly Vietnam, may be the greatest debt of all.

One of the small restrictions the National Guard had imposed on me was in my choice of hairstyles. The Beatles had inspired kids around the world to let their hair grow long. Prior to the Beatles, most kids sported flat tops or crew cuts, or if you were a "non-conformist" and you were really daring in the 50s you wore your hair in a DA, short for a "duck's ass," or ducktail cut. After the Beatles, especially in the music business, if you *didn't* have long hair you were considered a square or weird. It was a complete turnaround. People in the music and entertainment business led the charge.

As a military man having to go to reserve meetings regularly, I had to wear my hair very short. People I dealt with in the business would ask me, "Why do you wear your hair so short?" I felt weird with short hair. I was still in the military and would be until I turned 32, but now that I didn't have to attend Reserve meetings I could wear my hair longer, grow sideburns and a mustache and I did. That was one of the side benefits of meeting the Sergeant.

In spite of the fact the dance at the Fairmont Armory had been a box office loser, my chance meeting with that Sergeant turned out to be one of the greatest things that ever happened to me, and that made my $600 financial loss on the Fairmont dance well worth it. I was down $1,200 so far for the week when I thought I would be up $6,000, but I was celebrating my release from Reserve meetings.

The next night we played Clarksburg West Virginia. I felt much better about working Clarksburg because my friend Nicky Corvello was the all-night jock at Clarksburg's WBOY radio station. The owners of a local restaurant had constructed a 20-foor transmission tower and broadcast studio right in the middle of their parking. Nicky played records all night from that elevated studio. It was a huge local attraction and very popular with the kids. They would hang out in the parking lot chowing down on hamburgers and malts, blaring Nicky's broadcast from their car radios. It was like a scene from George Lucas's classic film *American Graffiti*.

I had become friends with Nicky when he was on the air at WHJB in Greensburg PA, near my hometown of Trafford. He was always willing to play any record I brought to him.

After the Fairmont show, Dickey Lee and the band wanted to check into a local motel to sleep. I suggested to Mike, Charlie and Sonny that we drive on to Clarksburg and get a motel there instead. It was only a ninety minute drive.

"What do you want to do that for?" Charlie complained.

"We lost money tonight and we lost money last night. If we keep losing and you keep paying for our rooms and our meals you're going to go broke. We can sleep in the car and wash up when we go to the dressing room at the armory. We can even get some sleep there before the show. You don't need to spend any more money right now on us."

He had a point. So we slept in the car and settled on cheap hot dogs for dinner. We agreed to pay for motel rooms only when we made money. That's why I loved Charlie.

The shows went on like this for the remainder of the week. We lost money in every city except good old reliable Conneaut Lake Park. Instead of the $21,000 profit for the week I had hoped for, I lost more than $1,000, even with the $3,000 profit from the Conneaut Lake show. I was broke again but I still had next week booked with Jimmy Soul as the headliner. Dickey Lee, bless his heart, felt responsible for my loss and offered to give back $375, which was half of his guarantee. But I wouldn't take it.

The Second Week: Jimmy Soul

Jimmy Soul, whose real name was James McCleese, grew up in North Carolina and like a lot of black entertainers he started out singing gospel music in his church. He had two hits before I booked him to follow up the Dickey Lee fiasco. "Twistin' Matilda" hit the charts three years earlier, but his big hit was "If you Wanna Be Happy," which sold over a million records two years earlier and was still getting a lot of airplay. I thought we would do much better with Jimmy and optimistically projected that we would hit our $21,000 profit goal for the week. I told Mike, Charlie, and Sonny, "I appreciate the sacrifices you made last week, but this week is going to be much better. This week we will all get to stay in motels and eat real food. And if we do really well, you'll all get a bonus."

Jimmy arrived in Pittsburgh on Sunday night the day before the first show in Johnstown. He stayed in my apartment instead of staying in my office next door like Dickey. He didn't like being alone. He wanted to talk. So he kept me up all night discussing his thoughts about show business. He wanted to become a bigger star. He had a plan and I was actually impressed with it. He complained about his manager and his record company and the fact that he had sold a million records but had made no money. I was paying him $750 for the week and out of that, he explained, he had to pay his agent and his manager. His net would be only about $500 and from that he would have to pay his living expenses at home, as well as his road expenses. "I just can't make it on that," he said.

"You sold a million records! You should have made a lot of money," I said.

"Are you kidding? I didn't make anything. I've never been paid."

It was hard for me to believe that a recording artist like Jimmy could sell a million records and not make any money, but then, the record business was full of crooks.

As he sat on the floor, Jimmy tapped his fingers on my coffee table and began to sing. Then he stopped and looked directly at me. "I have a hit in my head," he said. "Listen to this song. You know the song but, I want you to listen to the way I do it. Listen to the rhythm. I'm trusting in you not to give this song to anyone else. Do you hear me?" Continuing to tap his fingers, he sang his version of the George Gershwin song "Summertime." When he was done, he looked at me and said, "Well?"

I replied, "Yeah. I think it is great! It's a hit. When are you recording it?"

"I'm not!"

"What do you mean? Why not?"

"My record company and my manager don't like it and won't record it. I want you to record it. I want you to be my manager."

"Jimmy," I said, "I have a record label and I do a lot of recording, but you already have a manager and you are already signed to a label. How could I record you?"

"It's simple," Jimmy said, "I'll record under a different

name. Let's make up a name right now. No one has to know about this but us."

"Jimmy, you can't do that. Go to your manager and your label and tell them you're not satisfied and things need to change."

"I can't. I need you to help me. Can you talk to them for me? I want to be big, really big, and I could be big if things were different."

"If what was different?" I asked.

"I could be big if I was white. I often think and ask God why did you make me black? You're white, Pat, and you live up North. You don't know what it's like being black in the South. You don't know what it feels like being called "nigger." I can't even eat where you eat or stay in the same hotel with you in the South. DJ's don't play many records by blacks. They play the white versions. You know that as well as I do and you know what, there's not a damn thing I can do about it."

Jimmy was right—white acts had all the advantages and could make more money. I was empathetic because growing up I was sometimes mistreated just because I was poor and Italian. I remembered, too, when Miss Bierer, my English teacher, told me that I should relinquish my position as President of the National Forensic League because she thought someone else was more deserving than me. So yes, I could empathize, but how could I ever really know what it was like to be black in a white society?

I also remembered The Marcels, a mixed black and white group from Pittsburgh who had a huge hit record with "Blue Moon," telling me how difficult it was for them in the South because of the race issue. Just as Jimmy was telling me, the black guys in the group had to stay in different hotels and they couldn't eat in the same restaurants or use the same restrooms as the white members of the group.

A hillbilly from West Virginia once called me a "black dago." I was 18 at the time and living in New York. We were both working for Tim at Mobile Records. He was twice as big as me and I lashed out at him when he called me that. He hit me and I bounced off the wall onto the floor, then he jumped on me and pinned me down, punching me in the face. He would have beaten me to a pulp if Tim and the rest of the guys hadn't pulled him away. Calling me a black dago was a morbid insult and it hurt bad. To feel that hurt every day, as Jimmy did, would be intolerable.

"I tell you what, Jimmy, let's get through this week and see how things look. We'll talk about it and keep in touch." At that point I excused myself to make a personal call in my office next door. I had to break away for a while from Jimmy and his depression.

A half hour later, when I returned, I detected a unique odor in the living room where Jimmy was sitting. I saw smoke coming from a bowl on the coffee table and a funny looking cigarette in his hand. "What's that smell?" I asked.

"Incense, smells good doesn't it?" He said.

"I don't know. I have allergies and all that stuff bothers me."

"Well, I guess you don't want this?" He said as he handed me the funny looking cigarette.

"No, thanks I don't smoke."

I was still a little naïve, I suppose. I thought it was just a hand rolled cigarette.

We started off the tour again in Johnstown, Pa. The crowd this time was little bigger and a little different. Jimmy's big hit, "If You Wanna Be Happy," was a raucous party song, unlike Dickey Lee's records, so the kids had come ready to rock. It was a much better show.

But all my optimistic projections for the week were once again dashed. I lost money all week, including the $3,000 I would have made had I just played Conneaut Lake Park and none of the other shows. I couldn't carry on for the whole summer like that. So I got smart and canceled the next two mini-tours we had already booked and scratched the whole summer's worth of bookings. It was an idea that just didn't work.

I did keep in touch with Jimmy. He called several times

and kept trying to persuade me to record his version of "Summertime." I believed his treatment of the song had hit potential and I would have recorded it, but I just couldn't do it, not the way he wanted to do it. He asked me again to talk to his record company and get a better deal for him. I told him that I would be willing to talk to his manager, but I didn't think it was appropriate to talk to his recording company first. Eventually, I guess, Jimmy gave up on me because he quit calling. I never heard from him again.

Several months later, in 1966, Billy Stewart released a version of "Summertime" that was very much like Jimmy's and it became a Top Ten hit on Chess Records out of Chicago. Jimmy was right about the song being a hit, but he never got to record it himself. I never did find out why or what happened. Jimmy suffered the plague of so many recording artists that come and go—he never had another hit. He quit the entertainment business and joined the Army. In 1988, Jimmy died of a heart attack. He was 45.

Like Jimmy, Billy Stewart had no follow up to his only hit, either. A few years later he was killed when his car plunged over a bridge into a river, just two months prior to his 33rd birthday.

I learned more about life and business during that two week mini-tour disaster than I had ever learned at any other time in my life. Throughout my career to that point I had been obsessed by the desire for hit records, not only for myself, but also for the artists I recorded and managed. I thought if I only had hits, if I only had gold records on my wall that alone would make me successful. I would have it made. But that was not necessarily true. Here I was promoting stars who had million selling records and yet they were not happy and they still had no money. I would come to learn in the years ahead that even the biggest stars suffer from profound insecurity. They all worry about that next release and then the one after that and then the next one and it goes on and on and on. They worry about getting older, getting fatter, and they constantly worry if they will still have an audience to love them tomorrow.

In order to cope with this day-to-day insecurity, many artists turned to drugs for relief. Many of the most successful groups were so torn by fragile egos they couldn't even get along with each other. There was jealousy over who the star of the group really was. Drugs and egos and insecurity tore apart many great acts back then, and even still today.

I learned success cannot be measured by material things. It cannot be measured by the number of gold records on your wall. Big stars have it all, fame, fortune, good looks, you name it, yet few of them seem to be truly happy.

Sammy Davis Jr., who suffered his own share of racial problems and insecurities, was right when he said, "I'm the show and you're the business." Ultimately, that's where I chose to be—in the business side of show business. I never had to worry about coming up with that next big hit. All I needed to know was who *did* have that big hit and then buy the act.

I drew no paycheck for my summer mini-tour and I had no one to blame but myself. Sure I lost money on it, but I was doing something I loved to do and how many people get a chance to do something for a living they really love to do? Not many people in this world do what I do or even could do what I do if they tried, I reasoned, so even when I lost money, as I did on that tour, I was not a loser. And I never would be.

Chapter Thirteen
The Stanley Theater

Buying the Stanley Theater 1977

By 1977 I had grown weary of the business, the egos, and the pressure. I couldn't get myself to go into my office and was spending most of my days at home working on my farm about 20 miles east of Pittsburgh. My brother Joe would call nearly every day and admonish me, "You'd better get yourself into that office and tend to those shows or you're not going to have a business left." I knew he was right and that he was just thinking of my best interests, but I felt more comfortable on a tractor and working with my animals than I did working with egotistical rock stars, demanding booking agents and unreasonable building managers.

I formed a partnership with Pittsburgh booking agent Rich Engler in 1973 and amended the name of the company to become DiCesare-Engler Productions. Rich lifted much of the burden of day-to-day booking chores off my shoulders so I could focus more on managing the venues themselves and mainly acquiring theatres and other real estate. I was good at this and loved it. Tim Tormey taught me early on in the business that to maintain long-term success in the concert business you had to control the real estate, i.e., the venues.

He griped that artists would never be loyal to any one promoter. He called them all "whores."

"It's not like the old days anymore," he said. "When we did a favor for an act by getting their record played or getting them a play day, they remembered and appreciated you forever. Now it's "Don't tell me what you did for me yesterday, tell me what you you're going to do for me *now*."

I had a good working relationship with the managers of the Syria Mosque, the Arena, and the Stadium. They all respected me. I focused on our relationships with them and because Rich understood what the audience liked to see, especially the younger audiences, he focused on the artists and bookings. Between the two of us we had everything covered. We were a good team.

I had to drive into Pittsburgh one day, which I didn't do much anymore and didn't really want to. Most days I stayed on the farm and did business with Rich over the phone. I had faith in his judgment and I trusted him. There was no need to drive into the office each day.

But on this day I had to. On my way in I happened to drive past the Stanley Theatre and noticed that the marquee said, "Open Fri, Sat, and Sun only." I wondered, why is this theater open only on weekends? The Stanley was one of Pittsburgh's premier movie theaters and it could seat 3,400 patrons. The thought came to me from out of the blue—if I owned the Stanley, I could control the concert business in Pittsburgh.

The reason for this was simple—every artist manager knows the way to build his act is to start out playing small clubs, work up to small theaters, and if the hits followed, build it into a stadium act. Very few acts get to the stadium level, but they all start out at the club and theatre level. If I could offer a prestigious venue like the Stanley to hot up-and-coming acts it would give us a great new niche in Pittsburgh no other promoter could compete with. When those acts rose to superstardom, who do you think would get first crack at promoting them in Pittsburgh?

Fired up by the idea, I parked the car to take a closer look at the place, wondering if it could possibly be for sale, how much it might be worth, and where I might get the money to buy it if it was. I walked around the exterior of the entire building and crossed the street to view the building from different angles. It was perfect for DiCesare-Engler. I wanted it. I've been lucky all my life. Whenever I needed money, the money materialized. I don't know how or why, but it did. At that moment I had no idea how the money I would need to buy the Stanley Theater would materialize. I didn't even know if was for sale, but my instincts told me to go for it.

The theater was closed so I peered through the glass of the front doors and spotted a black man inside who appeared to be cleaning. I knocked on the door to attract his attention. Through the glass he shouted "We are closed, come back on Friday."

"I'm here to see the theatre because I'm going to buy it," I shouted back, "I'll only be a minute."

He opened the door and said, "I shouldn't do this. I'll get fired if my boss hears about this."

As I walked through the door into the theater a second cleaning person—a black woman—approached me. "Who are you and what are you doing here?" she inquired politely.

"My name is Pat DiCesare. I am interested in buying this theatre and when I do I want you both to work for me. A theater as beautiful as this should be open every night." I said.

"Mr. Pat, I'm Ollie and this is my man Willie, and you're right. We've been cleaning this theater for years. When it first opened in the late twenties every big singer in the country would perform on this stage every night before the movies started. It's a shame how things changed. Now it is only opened on the weekends. It's disgraceful."

They showed me around the interior of the theater with obvious pride, as if it were their own. It was decorated throughout with exquisite marble, plush carpeting, and huge glass chandeliers and I saw no reason why The Stanley Theater could not become the crown jewel of the city once again.

Willie and Ollie kindly provided me with the owner's contact information. "Don't forget us when you buy this place, Mr. Pat." I promised them, "Of course I won't!"

There were two other theaters in Pittsburgh we had used in the past—Heinz Hall was a world-class venue but they did not want rock concerts, and even though the Syria Mosque could rightly be called the birthplace of rock concerts in the city, I hated dealing with Miss Steele, who didn't like having rock shows at her theater any more than they did at Heinz Hall and dealing with her made my life miserable. Another drawback was that the Mosque had no air conditioning, so summer shows were uncomfortable for the fans, whereas the Stanley did.

The Stanley, as I learned from Willie and Ollie, was part of the Cinemette chain of theaters owned by Tom Reich and John Harper. Harper was a graduate of the prestigious Wharton School of Business and his father was the president and CEO of Alcoa, headquartered in Pittsburgh, and Tom was an attorney who represented professional athletes as an agent. John was a hard man to reach. After getting nowhere for a few days with his secretary/gatekeeper, I took the bull by the horns and walked into his office unannounced, without an appointment.

"I'm Pat DiCesare here to see Mr. Harper," I told the receptionist.

"Do you have an appointment?"

"No, but please let him know that I am here to see him. I want to buy the Stanley Theatre."

That did the trick. A few minutes later I was ushered into John Harper's office. His first words were, "Hello, Pat DiCesare, are you the guy that does all the concerts in town?"

"Yes I am."

"What makes you think the Stanley Theater is for sale, Mr. DiCesare?"

"Well sir, the marquee says it's open only on weekends. Movie theaters like the Stanley are losing business all across this country to shopping mall theaters with multiple screens.

You're getting hit by a 10% amusement tax and your customers are getting hit by parking fees. Soon, there will be more movie theaters like the Stanley going out of business. It's just a matter of time."

"That may be true, sir," he answered, "But the Stanley is not for sale. Now if you'll excuse me, I have a meeting in ten minutes." And with that I was ushered right back out.

I had been shot down, but I knew in my heart that my assessment of Mr. Harper's industry was right and that the Stanley Theater was right for DiCesare-Engler, so I was not about to give up that easily. Six months later, in January 1977, I called on John Harper again. "I still want to buy the Stanley Theater," I told him.

This time, I was *not* ushered out of the office immediately. Instead he said, "Okay. What are you offering?" Obviously, things had changed at Cinemette Theaters.

"What are you asking?"

"Two point five million."

Two point five million! How would I ever pay that? As usual, I had no idea how I would get the money I needed and I had two point five million questions, but somehow I *knew* that I could make it happen. I was not about to let this deal slip through my fingers now. But neither was I about to accept his first offer.

"It's not worth two-and-a-half million, Mr. Harper."

And with that, we entered into negotiations that took six long months, but in the end, DiCesare-Engler came to own The Stanley Theater, not for Harper's first $2.5 million asking price, but for only $1.1 million.

As I expected, the money materialized when I needed. It's amazing what you can do with a little creative financing when you are determined enough…and I was. The deal was not without risks, and there was an enormous amount of red tape to work through. We had city ordinances to get around, a liquor license to secure, and a cash down payment to make. But that is always the case in purchases like this. As Tim Tormey so often said, "If you wait until you have the money to do something, you will never do anything."

Upon closing the deal, the first two people I hired for our new theater, as I had promised, were the two janitors, Ollie and Willie.

Thus, a new era for DiCesare-Engler Productions began. Our first concert in September 1977 featured jazz great, Al Jarreau. It was a sellosut. The following year, *Billboard Magazine* named the Stanley as the number one theatre in the country in its class—under 4,000 seats. Its success exceeded our own expectations. The Stanley Theater was a hit.

Selling the Stanley Theater: 1984

The Stanley years were the greatest years of my life. I wish that everyone could have the opportunity to experience what all of us who were involved with The Stanley experienced. I wanted that part of my life to go on forever, but when I was presented with the opportunity to sell the theater in 1984 at an enormous profit I thought of all the things I could accomplish with the money and it was too much to resist.

So on June 14, 1984, after a successful seven-year run of sold-out shows, we sold the Stanley Theatre. It was emotionally painful, but the reality was that as the concert business continued to get bigger and as the acts got bigger they, and their agents, started looking for bigger paydays, and that meant playing bigger venues. Years earlier, a similar pattern of growth had led to the demise of classic 50s night clubs like the Holiday House. The demand outstripped the capacity of the venues. Toward the end of our run with the Stanley Theater the biggest acts were asking for guarantees of a hundred thousand dollars a night and that was simply impossible to meet with a theatre of only 3,400 seats without raising ticket prices beyond the public's willingness to pay.

The time was right to sell. I didn't realize it then, but selling the Stanley was the beginning of the end for me in the concert business. The final curtain would drop in 1999 with the sale of DiCesare Engler to SFX. I never wanted that sale to happen, either, but again it was all about money—big money—and again, it was too hard to resist.

Today things are different.

The concert business was no longer operating the way it did when I started with Tim Tormey over fifty years earlier. Performers were demanding unheard-of guarantees and it was the age of the conglomerates. Huge corporations were taking over all sorts of independent businesses through mergers and acquisitions and they had focused their attention on the entertainment business. I knew it was time for me to get out. I did not want to be a part of the company that was buying us. Other than my early years working for Tim Tormey, I had never worked for anyone else in this business and I wasn't about to start now.

Yes, the business was changing. At DiCesare-Engler, we cared about our audience. We were concerned about keeping our ticket prices low and so were the artists. But things had become much less personal and much more cutthroat. It had become corporate.

When SFX was negotiating to buy DiCesare-Engler we had to agree to turn all of our bookings over to them at the closing. Rich was working on two dates at the Civic Arena for Janet Jackson. Her agent wanted a guarantee of $350,000 a night against a large percentage of the gate, whichever was greater. Rich negotiated the agent down to a guarantee of only $250,000 a night, a savings to us of $200,000 over the two day period. But at the closing, SFX told us they didn't want the deal for $250,000. They were willing to pay the $350,000 per night that Jackson's agent originally asked for.

"Why in the world would you give back a $200,000 concession?" we asked. Their answer was they wanted both the acts and their agents to know SFX would not negotiate the price of the act down. They would pay the acts whatever price they demanded. They wouldn't even negotiate!

Immediately, the ticket prices we fought so hard to hold down all those years went through the roof. The agents knew that promotion companies, which were now mostly owned by large corporations, were willing to throw big money at the acts. It was crazy! Soon, artists were asking for a million dollars a night guarantees and the large corporations were paying it! But it wasn't like it had been with me throughout my career. This was stockholder money. No one was risking their own personal money anymore.

Consequently, ticket prices kept increasing and all these new corporate promoters didn't care. Tickets were no longer ten, twenty, or thirty dollars. They were now one, two, and three *hundred* dollars.

Throughout my career I had always made sure that our employees felt special, like they were part of the family. So they took personal pride in every show. Today, onsite employees are nobodies. They're numbers. They get no special treatment. They are part of no family. They feel no personal pride in the shows they work. It's just a job. And I believe it shows in the overall concert experience for the fans. It's an intangible difference, but there is a difference, and not a particularly positive one.

At the Stanley Theatre, we had regular customers who attended almost all our shows. The Stanley was *the* place to be. People loved it, and area businesses supported us. They took care of our needs and we took care of them with tickets to our shows. Restaurants fed us. Clothing stores, car dealers, jewelers—they gave me just about anything I wanted. No charge. All they wanted were tickets to the shows and to be able claim they were sponsors of Pat DiCesare concerts. I took free vacations to Europe and Hawaii. I got free tickets to all the professional hockey, baseball, and football games in the city. I was a *somebody*.

Today it's different. When I go to a concert, I'm a nobody, too, and I have to stand in line, like everybody else. That old "scratch my back and I'll scratch yours" system that worked so well for me doesn't exist anymore. It's no longer personal. It's just business. Is that a good thing? Well, overall, ticket sales are down. Artist's tours are routinely cancelled these days due to a lack of sales. On the plus side, though, independent concert promoters have started springing up again and they are playing small acts at small facilities at reasonable prices. Artists are again becoming more sensitized to the desires of their fans. Lower ticket prices are again becoming the norm, except for a handful of superstars like the Rolling Stones and U2.

When I started out I was able to accomplish great goals with no money or schooling. Nobody was teaching the music business in colleges and universities. I learned from doing. Fortunately, I had a great mentor in Tim Tormey, but he was learning as he went along, as well. I give guys like Tim, Lenny Litman, and Alan Freed credit for creating the concert business as we know it today. *Nobody* taught those guys how to operate the concert business, but they taught me.

Although there were plenty of competitors in the late 1950s the business was wide open and ready for the picking if you knew what you were doing. I was blessed somehow to understand rock and pop music and what people wanted. But there wasn't as much variety in music then as there is today. There was some folk, some jazz, and some country, but most of all, there was rock and roll. Today there are many different genres of music and many different niche markets. And that's a good thing because that is what is now fueling the resurgence of independent concert promoters and lower ticket prices.

DiCesare-Engler in Pittsburgh, Bill Graham in San Francisco, the Belkin Brothers in Cleveland, Sid Bernstein in New York, Larry Magid and Alan Spivak in Philadelphia, Berry Fey in Denver—we all started out in back rooms with no money and no roadmaps. We were pioneers carving out a new industry with a new breed of recording artist. Most of us had worked in the record business, the talent agency business, or we had ourselves produced records and managed recording acts, and all this experience combined to make us the first generation of rock concert promoters. We knew what the fans wanted to hear *in our own hometowns,* both on vinyl and in concert venues, and we gave them what they wanted. We were impresarios and ambassadors for the music business. It was revolutionary and exciting, and it was an era of popular culture that will never happen again.

In today's big corporate promotion companies the decision makers don't live in the cities they're booking. Everything they know of the fans in those cities is written in numbers. Everything is consolidated. The same thing has happened with radio. Radio station owners, who were once limited by law to owning only a few stations, can now own as many as they can afford to buy. This has led to tighter play lists, which limits air play for new artists. Ticket agencies and even T-shirt companies have been bought and consolidated. Nothing is personal anymore.

In the case of DiCesare-Engler, we were first approached for buyout by Pace Concerts in Houston, who then made a deal with SFX, which was then purchased by Clear Channel, and was then finally spun off into what is now the biggest concert promotion company in the world, LiveNation. The record industry itself has fallen prey to corporate conglomeration, too. At one time, there were hundreds of independent record labels like Atlantic, Mercury, Stax-Volt, and Roulette, and these labels were responsible for countless hit records that are now considered to be timeless classics. You can credit Steve Jobs and Apple's iTunes for fueling the end of the record industry as we once knew it and, some say, the end of *real* music and real artists as we once knew them. Today, there are only three major record labels in the entire free world!

Another unfortunate byproduct of corporate takeovers is that smaller markets like Jackson, Mississippi or Harrisburg, Pennsylvania or El Paso, Texas don't get many significant concert acts anymore. Their music fans have to travel, sometimes hundreds of miles, to see a major concert. In my day, agencies would tour an act and kept them on the road for weeks, routing them through big towns and small towns alike. Not so anymore.

I often hear young people talk about opening new venues, and some of them do. We have no shortage of venues, what we have is a shortage of good acts who can sell out the venues that exist. We have a shortage of radio stations that will take a chance and play new music by new artists. We have a shortage of record companies who will gamble on spending their money in the studios and for marketing their new acts. Whereas a record company would once break new artists virtually every week, now they may break less than a half-dozen new artists all year. And if their first album doesn't go triple platinum, they don't get a second one. It's very tough now for new hopefuls hoping to be heard and hoping to be signed.

In 1999, the sale of DiCesare-Engler to SFX marked the end of my career in the entertainment business. The company I had started almost 40 years ago, ultimately made me a millionaire by the time it was sold. Now...it was all over for me but the memories.

There is only one thing I wish I could do all over again. I wish I could sit at the kitchen table with Mum and Dad again and slide another envelope to my mother. This time, instead of a check for $5,000 that made that first Beatles concert possible, it would be a check for $500,000. I would love to see the expression on her face.

I would love to say to my Dad, "I'm sorry I didn't take better care of the violin. Thanks for giving it to me. Thanks for the accordion lessons, and of course, thanks the $5,000 for The Beatles. And Mum, I *did* become a school teacher eventually, even if it was only for a year."

The Curtain Falls

Advancements have brought changes not only to me, but to the people and places in my life, as well. The grade school where I took my first violin lesson is gone. The high school where Miss Bierer took away my chance to lead my debate team is gone. Jay Michael, the DJ from WCAE who went out of his way to introduce me to the record companies, is gone. Joe Averbach, the man who started it all for me by having the Del Vikings record my songs and introducing me to Tim Tormey, is gone. Tim Tormey, my mentor, the man who believed in me and gave so many opportunities when I was starting out, is gone. The Holiday House Supper club, where I discovered my love for the business, is gone. Its owner, Johnny Bertera, is gone. Pete Tambellini and Zeke Nicholas, who booked the Penn Boys' first performances, are gone. The Syria Mosque, which stood for a hundred years, is gone. And perhaps worst of all, the landmark Civic Arena, where we introduced the Mega Concerts and where The Beatles performed in 1964, is gone, demolished in 2012 and replaced by The Consol Energy Center.

Even Three Rivers Stadium, where I produced my first ball park concert in 1971, has been demolished and replaced by two stadiums: Heinz Field for the Pittsburgh Steelers, and PNC Park for the Pirates. I am happy to say, however, that both fields are now being used as concert venues, as well.

But I am still here, and this has been the story of my life. I was not just a record guy and I was not just a concert promoter. I was a gambler. That's what this business is—one big gamble. I have made fortunes and I have lost fortunes, but if I had the chance to do it all over again, I would do it all the same way.

People often ask me, "What was it like working with all of those famous stars through all those years?" I always tell them, "They were hard days and hard nights, but they were the best days of my life."

Stones Rock Record Arena Crowd

By AL DONALSON
and
JACK GROCHOT

An electrifying Mick Jagger and his Rolling Stones turned on the musical heat last night, providing a hot time for thousands of fans at the Civic Arena.

"Ah, b r o w n sugah, how come you taste so good?" wailed the lead singer of the popular British rock group, while city police outside tried to cool disturbances.

The record crowd — 13,845 young people — reacted in ecstasy equal to the Stones' hard-rock rythyms under the silver dome last night.

The blaring music and the singing of Jagger, cavorting like a peacock in his skin-tight purple jump suit, kept those able to gain admittance oblivious to the occurrences outside.

Several hundred fans failed to heed earlier notices of a sellout and milled about the arena, causing scattered incidents of trouble for police.

As a result, about 70 young people were arrested, mostly

(Cont'd on Page 16, Column 2)

204

Afterword

By late 1973 something in me had snapped. I was promoting every arena and stadium concert in the tri-state area, managed most of the major acts in Pittsburgh, and produced records. I also owned an amusement park, restaurant, theatre, and was raising a family. My dreams had become reality, my businesses were thriving, but I was burning out fast. I worked seven days a week from 6:00 am to 1:00 am and I just wanted to quit.

I was the concert industry in the city of Pittsburgh. I had no real competition. There were many promoters who tried to move in, but they couldn't get any of the big acts or venues from me. I realized early in the business that the only way to control the acts was to have an exclusive on the real estate and I had all the venues wrapped up. If you wanted to play Pittsburgh, you worked with me. I knew I couldn't walk away from the business I worked tirelessly to build.

I needed a partner. Someone who understood the music, was willing to work my hours, and could be taught to do shows my way. This was a golden opportunity for the right person.

In November of 1973 I found Rich Engler and took him on as a partner. I imparted my knowledge of the business, how to book acts, manage shows, and be a successful promoter. Rich was eager and took to my direction.

I spent a few years away from the office, bought a small farm, and became interested in agriculture. I returned to the business in 1977 when I orchestrated the purchase of the Stanley Theatre. We made history by bringing some of biggest names in the music industry to Pittsburgh and was quickly named the number one rock venue in the country by *Billboard Magazine*.

DICESARE·ENGLER
Presents in the
Only Area Appearance

OZZY OSBOURNE

Special Guest **METALLICA**

SAT. APRIL 12, 7:30

at the
JOHNSTOWN
WAR MEMORIAL

Advanced Tickets at
National Record Mart

PRICE
$15.00589 SEC C13   C13 E   10 $15.0011045

SED ROW SEAT CHOICE SEAT
C13 E   10

$15.00 ADULT
PAID: ALL APPLICABLE TAXES INCLUDED

NO REFUND - NO EXCHANGE
AT RESELLER: RETURN TO PRINT
AT PURCHASE - REFUND IN EXCESS
PRICE PAID FOR BEYOND OF

1104552779   PAID

DICESARE-ENGLER PRESENTS
JOHN COUGAR MELLENCAMP
THE SCARECROW TOUR
PITTSBURGH CIVIC ARENA
THURS NOV 28 1985 7:30 PM
$15.00 ADULT A41   589527791A015001

Strohs   **DE** **DICESARE ENGLER**   *Strohs*

KENWOOD **Westwood One** PRESENT

FLEETWOOD MAC

WED., OCT. 14
7:30 pm
CIVIC ARENA

Special Guest
to be
announced

THE 19 *Tour* 87
FEATURING

Mick Fleetwood   **John McVie**   **Christine McVie**
Stevie Nicks   **Rick Vito**   **Billy Burnette**

TICKETS AT ALL "CHOICE SEAT" LOCATIONS INCLUDING KAUFMANN'S, HORNE'S,
RECORD OUTLET STORES and CIVIC ARENA, GATE #1.

TO CHARGE CALL 642-2067

Acknowledgments

Many thanks to everyone who believed in me, helped me, and to all those who became good friends over the last fifty years.

Kathy DiCesare, Patrick DiCesare, Dana, Damian, Jacob, Holly, Joe and Fran, Mike, Lucy Barzan, Chris Patchel, Kelly Ackerman, Chris Ulrich, Dick Roberts, Chris Grabowsky, Steve Acker, Gene Ciavarra, Monica Compton, Ed Traversari, Rich Engler, Al Murdoch, Alta and Frank Schollaert, Sharon Tomb, Dan Querio, Mellisa Querio, Judy and Jerry, Greta, John and Starr Mikan, Paul Mediate, Sonny Krupar, Sonny and Pam Vaccaro, Marty, Charlotte, Todd Gallagher, John Ciotti, Jim Vaccaro, John Shasko, Tony and Marsha Berardo, Chuck Corby, Elvira and Michael Pastel, Patricia Morocco, John Pavone, Anthony Berardo Jr., Phil Scrimenti, Rex Rutkowski, Scott Mervis, Chuck Brinkman, Tom Rooney, Jimmy Sacco, David Robinson, Jerry DeFabo, Tony DeNunzio, Vinny Sylvania, Harry Popovich, Lee Smalley, Jason Shapiro, Lucy Petrini, Herky Asquino, Paula, Joe Perry, Jeff Soltys, Judith Gallagher, Ron Bernacki, Fred Avolio, Jimmy and Carole Laspina, Rick Glauss, Barton Wooley, Helen Tormey, Dom, Ralph, Mick DiCesare, Cathy Teets, Michael Stienmetz, Gary Stiener, Jason Jack Miller, Heidi Ruby Miller, Joe Smetana, Brad Simmons, Ed Collins, Ken Meyer, J R McNiff, Joe Brown, Tony Morocco, Brock Malky, Dan and Linda Lattanzi, Larry Mastrovich, Vicky Krajewski, Mark Kovalcik, Ronn Scala, Barbara and Jack Kita, Bernie and Bill Katsur, Steve Juffe, Denise, Glenn, Josh Fischer, Bruce Huber, Rick Grannatti, Nick Geanopolis, Ken Garris, Vito and Lana DiSalvo, Dan Fussili, Dave Freeland, Joey DiSalvo, Cindy Yates, David Chen, Glen and Jackie Cavanaugh, Joe Carlucci, Vic and Cathy Capets, Linda and Bill Brewer, Mario, Karen and Danielle Tambellini, Joyce and Pat Harter, Jack, Jim and Becky Bombulie, Steve Bogacki, Roy Bodnar, Steve Aptor, William Allen